CAT·TALES

TRUE STORIES OF KINDNESS
AND COMPANIONSHIP WITH KITTIES

# CATTALES

ALINE ALEXANDER NEWMAN

WITH A FOREWORD BY
Mieshelle Nagelschneider, Cat Behaviorist

NATIONAL
GEOGRAPHIC

WASHINGTON, D.C.

# CONTENTS

# ASK AN **EXPERT**

Cats surprise us all the time. We marvel at their ability to find their way home, track down their favorite missing humans, or simply survive. Some of the feline wonders featured in this book have even saved human lives. You'll read their stories and think of questions—questions that can only be answered by an expert.

That's when you can turn to veterinarian Gary Weitzman for help. Dr. Weitzman is president and CEO of the San Diego Humane Society and SPCA. Throughout this book, he'll provide answers to some curious cat questions.

# FOREWORD

If you're looking for mystery, look no further than a cat! Cute and cuddly one minute and fierce and playful the next, cat behavior can seem harder to crack than the toughest code. Sadly, this lack of understanding between humans and cats can often lead to cats being left in shelters or given away from their homes due to "problem behaviors." But beneath their puzzling exteriors and sometimes frustrating antics, cats are wonderful creatures whose friendship is well worth the extra effort.

I've devoted my life to learning everything I can about domestic cats and their behavior, and helping owners make the best out of the relationships they have with their kitty companions. This work is incredibly important to me. Finding ways for cats and their owners to live harmoniously is not just a personal passion, it is also a method of saving lives. After many years of observing cats and studying animal cognition, I founded the Cat Behavior Clinic, which helps sometimes desperate owners find solutions to cats' most troubling behaviors.

The best way that owners can interact with their feline pets is to dive into the mind and the eyes of a cat. By creating an environment that appeals to a cat's wild instincts, owners can avoid most of the problems I see on a day-to-day basis at the Cat Behavior Clinic. Make sure your cat's home includes daily play times, vertical spaces to climb and explore, scratching areas, and food puzzles to keep things fun and interesting. Cats are not pack animals, so it is also important to provide enough litter boxes; I suggest one for each cat and an additional box. And most of all, remember that even a cat's most baffling actions often have simple solutions—crack the code and you will be on your way to becoming a feline phenomenon!

Cats have so much to offer—in return, they deserve a bit of effort on our parts to understand the behaviors that so often confuse us. Whether they are twitching their ears, meowing loudly, sitting right on our keyboards, or lazing in the sun, cats are always worth getting to know just a bit more.

—Mieshelle Nagelschneider
Founder, The Cat Behavior Clinic

AWESOME

# HOLLY

## AN INCREDIBLE JOURNEY

*Domestic Shorthair/Florida, U.S.A.*

Neither Bonnie nor Jacob Richter was concerned at first. Holly, their beloved indoor cat, had bolted out an open door before. Usually Holly spent a few minutes chasing away the harmless little lizards that skittered around all over Florida and then came back in. But one night, she scooted out and did not return.

The Richters had taken Holly with them, to a motor home rally, at Daytona International Speedway. So they were 190 miles (306 km) away from home, when she escaped from their RV. Maybe a booming fireworks display spooked her because, as Bonnie says, "We looked everywhere." She and Jacob notified animal rescue workers, had an

> A MICROCHIP IS A TINY, COMPUTERIZED ID TAG. A VET IMPLANTS IT UNDER A PET'S SKIN, WHERE IT CAN BE READ WITH A SCANNER. HAVING ONE HELPS PEOPLE RETURN LOST PETS TO THEIR OWNERS.

announcement made over the speedway's loudspeaker, and posted flyers. They even stayed two extra days searching for her. Still no Holly.

Distraught, the Richters finally headed home to West Palm Beach, Florida. "My husband cried all the way," Bonnie says.

The couple had never had a cat, until Holly padded into their carport one Christmas Eve. Inspired by the season, the Richters put out food and christened her Holly. And the grateful kitten stuck around. "She chose us," says Bonnie. That's important, because Holly was born feral, or wild. She feared people and hissed or ran away from everyone except Bonnie and Jacob.

Two weeks after Holly's disappearance, a Daytona rescue worker spotted her and called the Richters. They planned to drive back and get her, but Holly never showed up again.

Even so, Bonnie believed Holly would return. "People thought I was crazy," she says. "But I just had this feeling."

## JUST **FUR FUN**

In 1877, most people considered cats to be lazy good-for-nothings. Their reputation was so bad that an organization was formed in Belgium called the Society for the Elevation of the Domestic Cat. It was dedicated to finding useful things for cats to do.

Aware that cats possess an uncanny sense of direction, the society conducted an experiment. One April day, they stuffed 37 house cats into cloth bags and drove them via horse and buggy 20 miles (32 km) outside of town. There, they let their captives loose. One furry speed demon showed up back home in five hours flat! And all the cats had returned by the next day. Society members proposed that the government establish a postal service "manned" by cats!

Letter writers would bundle messages into bags and tie them around the necks of the mail cats. Then the cats would fan out over the countryside delivering them.

Would this scheme have worked? We'll never know, because the far-out idea was never put into practice. But it makes a pawsome tail, er, tale.

CAT MAIL

POSTCROSSING
5 CAT-MAIL
2013

ILFRACOMBE. LYNTON & LYNMOUTH. NEWTON

Jacob, however, was inconsolable. Every time he relaxed in his lounge chair, he longed to see Holly curled up on the footrest. He missed her so much that he wanted to get another cat.

"I wouldn't let him," says Bonnie. "We couldn't do that to Holly. When she came home, we couldn't have another cat in her place."

Then, just before New Year's Eve, a woman saw a scrawny cat too weak to meow staggering around in her Palm Beach backyard. She took the cat to a vet, who scanned it for a microchip.

The information on the chip led to Jacob, who gasped in disbelief when the pet registry called saying Holly had been found. What's more, she was within a mile (1.6 km) of home!

How had one little cat traveled 190 miles (306 km) in 62 days?

Apparently, she walked. "Her back paws were like hamburger, her nails were so ground down," says Bonnie. And the kitty had dropped six pounds (2.7 k), which was half her body weight.

As for how she found her way, nobody knows.

But this is what the Richters and an animal behaviorist think: The Richters' house is only five miles (8 km) from the Atlantic Ocean and half a mile (0.8 km) from Interstate Highway 95. From there it is a straight run up the coast, via I 95, to Daytona. Cats have super hearing and a powerful sense of smell. Holly would have been familiar with the traffic sounds and the smells of salt air and automobile exhaust. If she followed those sounds and smells back the way she came, she would have reached West Palm Beach eventually. "It was quite a trip for a little gal who really wanted to come home," says Jacob.

He and Bonnie hand-fed the exhausted kitty for weeks, to nurse her back to health. Today, Holly remains wary of strangers, but she follows her family everywhere. And she often sits on the dash of their motor home, when it's parked, and stares out the windshield. But this well-traveled cat with a big heart hasn't scooted outside once since coming home—not even to chase a lizard. ●

## ASK AN **EXPERT**

**Q:** How do you explain a cat tracking her owners to a new place, where the cat has never been?

**DR. WEITZMAN:** Cats are perfect hunters. Nature gave cats superior senses designed to help them track down prey. Some pet cats may be able to use those same senses to track down their people. Besides that, cats possess endless amounts of patience and persistence. Once on the trail of something, or someone, they keep going. They do not give up.

# SIMON

❀

## BATTLE CAT

*Domestic Shorthair/England, United Kingdom*

Inside the captain's cabin, on the British warship HMS *Amethyst*, a little black-and-white tomcat lay fast asleep. As usual, Simon was curled up in the captain's gold-braided hat. A 17-year-old British sailor had rescued Simon from Hong Kong's naval dockyards and smuggled him on board. Luckily for the sailor, the ship's captain took a special liking to the friendly feline, maybe because he proved to be an expert mouser. Hungry rats had infested the ship, and Simon caught at least one a day, often dropping his catch at the captain's feet. Months later, another captain took over the ship. He also loved Simon and doted on him as much as the first captain had.

ESTABLISHED IN 1943,
THE PDSA DICKIN MEDAL HAS BEEN
GIVEN OUT 68 TIMES TO 32 PIGEONS, 31 DOGS,
AND 4 HORSES. BUT ONLY ONE FELINE
HAS EVER WON IT—SEA CAT SIMON.

The year was 1948, and the communist revolution had turned mainland China into a war zone. Now the *Amethyst* was sailing up the Yangtze River to Nanking, to guard the British Embassy. But the unsuspecting crew sailed straight into an ambush.

Communist soldiers lined both sides of the riverbank. As the *Amethyst* steamed into view, the soldiers opened fire, resulting in numerous British casualties, including the captain. In the terrifying moments that followed, the ship ran aground.

With their ship burning and many sailors wounded, no one had time to look for Simon. Those who did think of him assumed he had died in the attack.

Finally, the firing stopped. The sailors maneuvered the ship off the sandbar, and the communists agreed to end their attack. But they refused to let the *Amethyst* leave. The communists were holding the beat-up vessel captive!

It was then that a sailor found Simon wobbling about in the debris. The captain's beloved cat, who used to amuse the men by scooping ice cubes out of a water jug with his paw, had survived! But his whiskers had been burned off. Both his back legs were slashed and bleeding. And he had sustained four shrapnel wounds. The sailor rushed the badly injured Simon to sick bay, where a doctor wrapped him in bandages.

Simon's fur grew back, and his wounds healed, but his heart had been permanently weakened. Despite that, he went right back to work catching rats. This mattered now more than ever, because being held captive meant that the ship couldn't replenish its food supplies. So the cooks couldn't afford to lose a single egg or an ounce of flour to a thieving rat. Without Simon's dedication, the sailors would have starved to death.

And that's not all. When he wasn't chasing rats, Simon visited the frightened teenage sailors lying in sick bay. He snuggled up to them on their bunks and inspired everyone with his loving devotion. If that little cat could endure the injuries he had suffered and not lose heart, the sailors figured they could do the same.

Under cover of darkness, on the 101st day of captivity, the crew restarted the ship and made a daring escape. When the battered *Amethyst* finally reached England, crowds of well-wishers turned out to cheer. Many came just to see the now famous hero cat.

But war hero or not, British law required that Simon be kept in quarantine for six months to be sure he carried no contagious diseases. While there, British citizens showered him with cards and letters and treated him with tins of sardines. Even so, the faithful kitty caught a virus that further damaged his already weakened heart, and he passed away a few short weeks later. But not before he was awarded the PDSA Dickin Medal for outstanding animal bravery under enemy fire. Today, a specially designed stone monument marks Simon's grave, in an animal cemetery in England. Folks who know the brave cat's story sometimes bring flowers and stand a moment, with bowed heads, to honor his memory. ●

# CORDUROY

## OLD FAITHFUL

*Maine Coon Mix/Oregon, U.S.A.*

Fifteen years. That's the average life span of a pet cat. But meet Corduroy. At age 26, or about 120 in human years, Corduroy has beaten the odds. The elderly cat has lost weight since his prime, but he still has all his teeth (few elderly humans do!), and he can leap from floor to counter in a single bound. This amazing supercat still patrols the 160-acre (65-ha) ranch in Sisters, Oregon, where he lives. And sometimes he even catches a mouse!

According to the *Guinness Book of World Records*, Corduroy is the oldest living cat in the world. But equally mind-blowing is the fact that he still lives with his original owner.

Ashley Reed Okura was not quite seven when her mother took her and her brother, William, to a fellow cat lover's house to pick out kittens. "We were so excited," Ashley said. "There were kittens on every surface."

The darling creatures appeared to be part Maine coon and part anybody's guess. Ashley and her brother chose two fluffy look-alikes that they christened Batman and Corduroy. Ashley named Corduroy after the stuffed bear in her favorite picture book.

Once home, Ashley dressed Corduroy in baby clothes, cradled him in her arms, and carried him around, like a human infant. From playdates to prom, Corduroy remained her fur-ever friend.

Then Ashley left for college. And 11-year-old Corduroy disappeared!

Besides their ranch, Ashley's family owned a large chunk of land in the Cascade Mountains. Maybe Corduroy was bored, or he missed Ashley, because he apparently stowed away in the bed of her father's pickup truck on one of his trips up there. Then the sneaky cat jumped out with nobody seeing. Not until nighttime, when Corduroy failed to

## JUST FUR FUN

Cats grow fast. It takes less than two years for a cat to reach adulthood. After that, they change more slowly, so that every human year equals about four cat years. From 7 to 14 years old, cats are middle-aged. They may act stiff, sleep more, and play less. Elderly cats, age 15 and over, will have lost weight and muscle mass. You can feel their backbone when you pet them. However, just like with people, good genes and a healthy lifestyle can make cats look and feel much younger than they are.

# WHO'S OLDER, YOU OR YOUR CAT?

| Cat's Age | Age in Human Years | Cat's Age | Age in Human Years |
|---|---|---|---|
| 1 year | 15 years | 9 years | 52 years |
| 2 years | 24 years | 10 years | 56 years |
| 3 years | 28 years | 11 years | 60 years |
| 4 years | 32 years | 12 years | 64 years |
| 5 years | 36 years | 13 years | 68 years |
| 6 years | 40 years | 14 years | 72 years |
| 7 years | 44 years | 15 years | 76 years |
| 8 years | 48 years | 16 years | 80 years |

*Gentle Corduroy looks ferocious playing with a pheasant feather given to him by Ashley.*

come in at home, did anyone notice him missing.

"Mom called me to break the news," said Ashley. "I was devastated, but I never really gave up hope."

A year passed. Then a family friend in the Cascades mentioned having seen a bobcat. "Are you sure?" Ashley's mom asked. "Please set out some food. If he comes again, see if he has a tail. If he does, it's Corduroy!"

Sure enough, days later, the friend stepped outside and scooped up Corduroy, who melted into her arms.

"I couldn't believe it!" Ashley said. "But he had the same notch in his left ear that he got as a kitten."

Corduroy, 12, was already nearing "retirement" age. How on earth had he managed to survive? Ashley thinks it's because she never had him declawed and always let him roam free. The exercise strengthened his muscles, and he developed excellent hunting skills.

Finally, safe at home, Corduroy resumed his old ways. He hung out with Batman and lounged in his favorite sunny alcove in the dining room.

Good thing, because disaster was about to strike. In 2005, Ashley's whole family was involved in a tragic accident that left her partially paralyzed.

Wracked by pain, Ashley endured years of surgery and rehabilitation. Through it all, her constant companion Corduroy, then 16, helped her feel secure.

"He followed me when I struggled to walk," says Ashley. "He slept beside me at night, and kept me company on the couch." She loved when he softly patted her face with his paw.

Through all the emotional events in her life, Corduroy has been at Ashley's side. The kitten she enjoyed dressing up when she was a little girl was still there 25 years later, when she got married. "It's been phenomenal," Ashley says. "I dread the day that he is not around anymore." Hopefully, that won't be anytime soon. Showered with love and devotion as Corduroy is, he may keep on breaking records. ●

# Maine **Coon**

🐾 **HOMELAND:** North America

🐾 **DISTINGUISHING FEATURES:** Gentle giants weighing up to 25 pounds (11 kg), with big, flat feet, a long plumed tail, and a ruff of fur around their neck

🐾 **WORTH KNOWING:** Unrelated to raccoons, Maine coons are one of America's most popular breeds.

# BAMBI

## QUIET TALK

*Siamese / Connecticut, U.S.A.*

"Meow. Meow." A woman fostering a houseful of rescued cats heard the pitiful cries. Glancing around, she saw all the cats were in the room with her. Except one. A newly arrived Siamese kitten was missing. A Good Samaritan had found the kitten hiding in a garage and took her to a Smart Animal Rescue in Spring, Texas, U.S.A. The rescue group had placed the kitten in foster care. Now the foster mother called to the little Siamese, but she didn't come. She just kept crying. So the woman checked on her and found the kitten all alone. The kitten acted scared, like she didn't know where the other cats went. And the reason she didn't know, the woman suddenly realized, was because she was deaf.

Kim Silva and her husband, John, are also deaf. So when they decided to get a new cat, they wanted one that was deaf, like them. To find one, Kim went online to a pet adoption site and checked the search box labeled "Special Needs."

And guess who showed up? It was the scared little kitten! Kim fell for her right away. She admired the touches of yellow, called "points," on her ears and the pretty yellow stripes on her tail. Most of all, she loved the alert look in the kitty's bright blue eyes, which Kim thought saw right into her heart.

When Kim offered to adopt her, the kitten was put on a bus full of rescued dogs and was driven to Connecticut.

While waiting for her to arrive, Kim began teaching American Sign Language (ASL) to one of her other cats, Bobcat. Bobcat could hear. But Kim hoped the deaf kitten, which she named Bambi, would learn from him. The first sign she taught Bobcat was "more."

To do it, Kim pinched some kibbles of dry cat food between her thumbs and fingertips. Then she held her hands out in front of her body, with her fingertips almost touching, and

*Bambi watches Kim's hands as Kim tells her "sit" by moving and resting two fingers of one hand over two fingers of the other.*

*Bambi eyes Kim's cup of yummy treats, while greeting Kim with a friendly pawshake.*

tapped her hands together. "[Bobcat] could smell the treats," says Kim. When he came toward her, she gave them to him. Kim worked with Bobcat every day, signing from chairs and tables, and always moving farther away. Bobcat quickly learned that every time he came, he got a treat.

Then Bambi finally arrived. Whenever Kim signed "more," Bobcat came running. So Bambi did the same and earned a treat, too.

Bambi and Bobcat seemed to enjoy learning to communicate so much that they began coming to class all on their own. They would jump up onto the kitchen desk and watch Kim, almost like they were eagerly waiting for Kim to "tell" them what to do.

Besides "more," Kim taught the duo other signs, including "up," "shake," "go-around," "sleep," "sit," and "stay." Teaching "stay" required a lot of patience. "It took a while before

I could leave the room, return, and the cats would stay," she says. But eventually they did.

Bambi even learned to sign back! When Kim makes the sign for "play," Bambi stretches up and taps Kim's signing hands with her paw. That means she wants Kim to crumple up a ball of paper and play with her. "Bambi chases the ball, plays fetch, and even jumps up and bats the ball back to me," says Kim. "I should have named her Soccer!"

Bambi enjoys a full life. And she never fails to show her appreciation. Whenever Kim signs that it's time to eat, Bambi jumps up and nuzzles Kim's hands before racing to her dish. "I think she's saying 'thank you,'" says Kim. If so, maybe she's grateful for the food. But maybe it's more than that. Maybe Bambi appreciates being able to "hear" what is being said. ●

# Siamese

 **HOMELAND:** Thailand (formerly Siam)

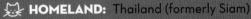 **DISTINGUISHING FEATURES:** Light-colored with dark-colored "points" on the face, ears, legs, and tail; slender, short-haired, and graceful

 **WORTH KNOWING:** Named for their native land, Siamese cats are "talkative" lap sitters who crave companionship and dislike being alone.

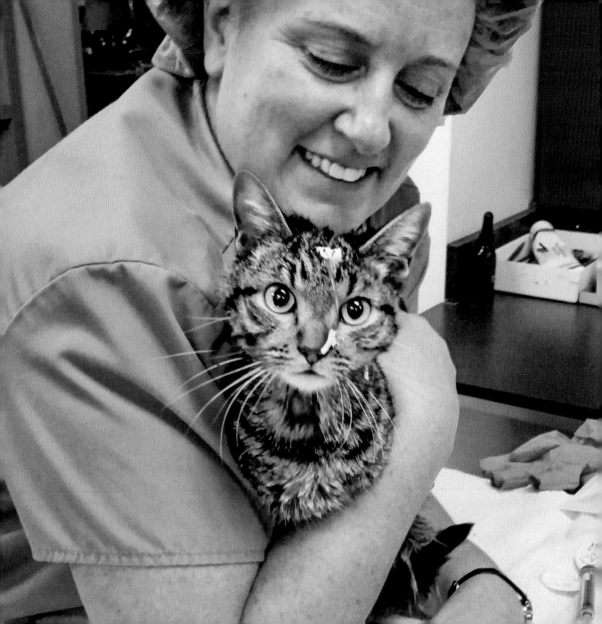

# MOOSIE

## OVERCOMING ALL ODDS
*Domestic Shorthair/Alaska, U.S.A.*

Moosie is one tough tabby. He started his life inside the wall of a house, in a military housing complex in El Paso, Texas. Apparently, a stray cat had entered through a gap in the roof and given birth to five kittens. Nobody knew the kittens were in the wall until the Army wife living there heard a faint meowing. She called the housing supervisor, who knocked a hole in the wall and found a sad sight. The mama cat and most of her kittens had died. But not Moosie! He was alive and crying to be fed.

Another Army family, Kymberly and Jesse Chelf, adopted the little survivor. Kymberly loved the way he hugged her neck and purred.

> **MOST CATS DISLIKE CHANGE.
> GET YOURS USED TO A NEW HOME
> BY SHUTTING HER IN ONE ROOM FOR
> SEVERAL DAYS BEFORE LETTING HER
> EXPLORE THE REST OF THE HOUSE.**

When Moosie was two years old, the Army transferred Jesse to far-off Fairbanks, Alaska. "It was such a stressful time," says Kymberly. The movers crammed the Chelfs' belongings into cardboard boxes, which were nailed inside wooden shipping crates. But the men left out the family's futon, so the Chelfs would have someplace to sleep.

When the movers returned to load the truck, Kymberly was home alone with Moosie; their other cat, named Milo; their dog, Misha; and their newborn baby, Lexie. "Hold on," Kymberly yelled, when the movers began propping open doors. "I haven't shut the cats in the bathroom yet." The men closed the doors and waited, while she searched for Moosie and Milo.

Kymberly found Milo right away, but Moosie had disappeared. He couldn't have crawled into one of the boxes, because the movers had taped them all shut two days before. And she had seen Moosie that morning. So where could he be? There seemed only one possible explanation.

"I assumed he ran out an open door," says Kymberly, who set out his food and kept going outside and calling his name. She even asked the movers to tip and shake the futon. Just in case. But Moosie failed to appear.

The men sealed the futon in a box and drove away. The Chelfs spent the next three days in a hotel and continued searching for their lost cat. But then they had to go. "It was very hard to leave without him," Kymberly says.

The heartbroken family drove to Alaska in ten days. But it took their stuff over two months to arrive. When it did, the movers unloaded the boxed-up futon last. As they did, Kymberly told them Moosie's story. The men sympathized and started carrying the futon upstairs. They had just reached the landing when they heard it. A meow! "I thought Milo was crying from inside the house," says Kymberly. Then she heard it again.

The movers stopped dead. "I think we found your cat," one of them said.

Jesse ripped open the box and pulled Moosie out. The poor animal must have gotten scared and clawed his way into the futon mattress to hide. Jesse rushed the kitty to Mt. McKinley Animal Hospital, where veterinarian Hayden Nevill took over his care. When Kymberly visited Moosie the next morning, she found him wrapped in a towel. He had lost most of his hair and all of his muscle. But not one bit of his fighting spirit! To Kymberly's great relief, he crawled over to her and tried to wrap his paws around her neck, like always.

After spending 64 days without food or water, Moosie needed help restarting his digestive system. The vet gave him IVs and a blood transfusion, and kept him on a feeding tube for a month. Hundreds of kindhearted people donated money to cover the bills. And today Moosie is fully recovered. "Miracles really do happen," says Kymberly. In Moosie's case, they happened twice. ●

# Celebrity
# CATS

Cute cats. Little cats. Cats that make us laugh. We adore them all and have even elevated some of them to superstar status. Whether real or imaginary, these fabulous felines stick in our minds and make us smile.

### GARFIELD

**TYPE:** Orange cartoon cat

**FAVORITE HANGOUT:** Everywhere

**CLAIM TO FAME:** This wisecracking cat has been making people laugh since 1978. Based on barn cats from Jim Davis's childhood, Garfield first appeared in newspaper comic strips. But he mouths off today in everything from books to television specials. And folks still call him lazy!

### FELICETTE

**TYPE:** Former Paris street cat

**FAVORITE HANGOUT:**
Outer space

**CLAIM TO FAME:** On October 18, 1963, this French feline became the world's first "astrocat." She was strapped into a capsule attached to a rocket and blasted into space for 15 minutes, while electrodes implanted in her head sent signals back to Earth. Scientists learned a lot, and she was safely recovered.

## LIL BUB

**TYPE:** Feline dwarf

**FAVORITE HANGOUT:** Online

**CLAIM TO FAME:** Known for her unusually cute appearance, Lil Bub is a viral sensation. Mike Bridavsky, who rescued the special needs cat that later helped him conquer depression, established Lil Bub's BIG Fund for the ASPCA, in 2014. Donations help pets needing special care.

## THE CAT IN THE HAT

**TYPE:** Fictional character

**FAVORITE HANGOUT:** Books

**CLAIM TO FAME:** This talking cat—who wears a tall, striped hat—was created by author Theodor Geisel, known as Dr. Seuss, in 1957. The funny feline played "lots of bad tricks" in two best-selling books. But his best trick has been helping over 12 million children learn to read.

## GRUMPY CAT

**TYPE:** Domestic shorthair

**FAVORITE HANGOUT:** Online

**CLAIM TO FAME:** In 2012, photos of Grumpy Cat's scowl appeared on the Internet. People began adding funny captions, which turned the photos into memes, and *wham!* A star was born. Grumpy's real name is Tardar Sauce, and grumpy she's not! Dwarfism, an inherited condition that causes short legs and a misshapen face, just makes her look that way.

CARING

# MONTY

## EVER WATCHFUL

*Domestic Shorthair/Alberta, Canada*

Patricia Peter had a cat. Now she wanted a kitten. The Edmonton Humane Society, about 64 miles (103 km) from her home in Camrose, Alberta, Canada, offered a special deal. You could adopt a kitten for free. So Patricia and a friend drove there. But by the time they arrived, all the kittens had been taken.

"I'll go look at the big cats," Patricia told her friend, disappointment sounding in her voice. In the big cat room, she saw two ladies playing with an ordinary-looking orange tabby. *Hmpff*, thought Patricia, who focused instead on a pretty Siamese. But the orange cat kept looking at her. Finally, Patricia picked him up. "He put his head right into

## CATS CAN SUFFER FROM DIABETES, TOO. IT IS MOST COMMON IN OLDER AND OVERWEIGHT CATS, AND SYMPTOMS INCLUDE OVEREATING, WEIGHT LOSS, INCREASED URINATION, AND EXCESSIVE THIRST.

my chest," she says. "We made eye contact, and my heart melted."

Patricia brought him home. He looked a lot like her other cat, Max, and she dubbed him "Monty." Lucky for all, Monty and Max got along. They enjoyed spending time outside together in the enormous, two-story-high dog kennel that Patricia keeps on her back deck. And Monty especially loved going camping with Patricia and her husband, Myron. Patricia often brought the kennel in the back of her pickup truck, so the cats could come.

The biggest difference between Monty and Max was Monty's affection for Patricia. "Monty was a very loving, one-person cat," Patricia says. "He was always by me." He met her at the door when she got home from work, and cuddled in her lap while she drank her coffee. When she went to bed, he curled up by her feet.

One night, six months after adopting him, Patricia was asleep when Monty suddenly bit her hand. "Ouch," she yelled, pushing him away. But Monty bit her again. The third time, she realized something was wrong. Her eyes seemed fuzzy, out of focus, and she started to sweat. "I stood up and almost passed out," Patricia says. "My whole body was shaking." She should have awakened her husband. But she was muddleheaded and stumbled to the kitchen instead. Monty walked beside her all the way, his body touching her left leg.

Patricia had been newly diagnosed with diabetes, and her medications weren't well regulated yet. She found her diabetes test kit on the kitchen counter and pricked her finger. Yikes! Her blood sugar level had dropped to 2.7! It should be between 4 and 8.

She drank a ginger ale, took a sugar pill, and lay down on the couch. Monty walked on her and refused to let her sleep. Fifteen minutes later, she retested her blood. Her

*Monty (left) looks like Max but doesn't act like him.*

It sounds divine—that wonderful rhythmic rumble of a pet cat's purr. But what does it mean?

Do cats only do it when they're happy? No. Cats purr for many reasons. They purr when they feel good, yes. But they also purr when they want company, either with another cat or their favorite human. And some tricky tabbies purr when they're hungry. These smarty-cats deliberately make their purr sound annoying, like a human baby crying, so that their person will hurry up and feed them. Perhaps most surprising is the fact that sick or injured cats sometimes purr.

There could be a good reason for this. A purr is caused by vibrations in the cat's larynx, or voice box. As that vibration spreads through the cat's body, it promotes bone growth. This means that if a cat injures her leg, purring might actually help it heal! More research needs to be done, but scientists are trying to invent a "purring" machine that does the same for us.

# PURR THERAPY

sugar level had returned to normal! "Monty saved me from going into a diabetic coma," says Patricia. He may even have saved her life.

But how did this untrained cat know Patricia needed help? A week later, Monty came into Patricia's sewing room and almost put his nose in her mouth. "My doctor said he was smelling my breath," says Patricia, who tested and found her sugar level low again. By smelling Patricia's breath, Monty could detect changes in her blood sugar before she could feel them herself. "Neither of my other cats have ever done this,"

*After four years, Monty's sweet stare still melts Patricia's heart.*

says Patricia, who now owns three. "Only Monty does it, and he has never been wrong!"

Patricia hasn't come that close to falling into a coma again. But in the last four years, Monty has sounded the alarm dozens of times. Once he warned Patricia three days in a row.

Monty's behavior was so extraordinary that he was inducted into the Purina Animal Hall of Fame, established in 1968, to honor animals that save human lives. Patricia and Myron flew to Toronto for the ceremony and saw Monty awarded a medal and a year's worth of free cat food.

"This cat was meant to look after you," Myron tells his wife.

And Patricia agrees. "I call Monty my guardian angel kitty," she says. If only every diabetic could have one. ●

# RUSSELL

## FROM GETTING HELP TO GIVING IT

*Manx/North Carolina, U.S.A.*

Some sick, hurt, or abandoned animals need a lot of caretaking. Other animals become caretakers themselves. Russell the ginger-colored Manx cat was both. In January 2014, Russell's home burned to the ground. The fire destroyed everything his human family owned and caused the death of two dearly loved pets—a dog and a cat. Leta Strickland, Russell's owner, was badly burned herself when she rushed back into the flames trying to save them.

Everyone thought Russell had died, too. But four days after the tragedy, Leta's adult daughter, Minerva, heard meowing in the rubble. She rushed to the sound and dug through the blackened debris with

**MANX CATS ARE BORN WITHOUT A TAIL. THEY FIRST APPEARED ON AN ISLAND NEAR GREAT BRITAIN ABOUT 300 YEARS AGO. ALMOST DOGLIKE IN THEIR DEVOTION, THEY LOVE FOLLOWING THEIR PEOPLE AROUND.**

her hands, until she found him. Russell's fur had all been singed off. He had serious burns covering most of his body. And his mouth, tongue, and ears were severely damaged. But he was breathing.

Minerva rushed Russell to Animal Emergency Hospital and Urgent Care, in Raleigh, North Carolina. "We had never seen an animal so badly burned," said veterinary technician Megan Maus. The vets thought they could save him, but he had to be sedated to relieve his pain. And he would need multiple surgeries and many months of burn treatments.

"This family had lost everything," Megan says. Not wanting them to lose Russell, too, the staff posted his story online. They hoped a few people would donate toward his care.

Instead, 40,000 people followed the story, and donations poured in from all 50 states and 40 foreign countries! Russell did his part, too. He endured all the pills, needle pokes, and painful dressing changes without complaint. "He was purring when they brought him in," says Megan. "And he purred his whole time here." Considering everything this

*A recovering Russell snuggles with Megan, after being disconnected from his IV machine.*
*Once free to move around, he trotted after staff members, meowing for attention.*

*Russell's badly burned ears
had to be amputated,
but that doesn't stop him from
cuddling with a toy sent by a fan.*

kitty went through, the lovable feline had every right to get grumpy, but he never did. Not once. "It was almost like he knew we were helping him," Megan says.

An intensive care animal hospital can be a loud, chaotic, and stressful place—for animals and humans. But Russell never seemed to let it get him down. Once off the IVs, the staff let him out of his cage. From then on, Russell slept in a comfy hammock made by one of his many online fans. It sat on the floor, against a wall, so Russell could wander freely between it and the staff room. If an employee was sad or upset, he snuggled with them until they felt better.

Russell did the same thing with nervous people sitting in the waiting room and with other four-legged sufferers. A homeless Chihuahua recovering from an animal attack especially needed help. So Russell let the frightened pup share his hammock.

Besides following Russell's progress online, people showered him with cards and gifts. One little girl donated her tooth fairy money, and a young boy wrote that reading Russell's story helped him and his hospitalized mom feel better.

So many packages arrived for Russell that he learned to recognize the *rrrrip* of employees tearing into boxes. "He would hear that sound and come running around the corner meowing," says Megan. Then he would sit and wait to see what toys or treats were inside.

Sometimes, of course, the boxes contained only medicine. But no matter. Russell never had to wait long. During his 18-month stay, half the mail the hospital received came addressed to the cuddly kitty.

In August 2015, Russell went back home to his family, who had since found a new home and had begun to rebuild their lives. Vets had amputated the tips of his ears, and parts of his face remained bald and stretched. But he could see and hear and run and play. The hospital staff misses him, but everyone is thrilled to see Russell and his owner, Leta, together again. ●

## ASK AN **EXPERT**

**Q:** What is the biggest misconception people have about cats?

**DR. WEITZMAN:** Many people think cats don't really care about us—that it's all about them. But that isn't true at all. Believe me, no self-respecting feline would put up with people just for food or treats. They care. They just show it differently.

# PUDDITAT

## CAT TO THE RESCUE

*Domestic Shorthair/Wales, United Kingdom*

An unusual cat with an unusual mission—that's Pudditat. This ordinary-looking gray-and-white house cat appears to be about 14. But nobody knows where or when he was born, or what his early life was like. The perceptive kitty suddenly showed up one day, on Judy Godfrey-Brown's doorstep, in Anglesey, North Wales.

Of all the houses in Judy's neighborhood, why did he pick hers? Maybe he had a sixth sense, because he could not have chosen better. "Judy was a real softie," says Anne Cragg, owner of Llangaffo Cattery, a boarding house for pets. The elderly animal lover already had five cats and one dog. So when Pudditat appeared, Judy opened the

door and welcomed him inside. At first, the new cat meandered around, sniffing everything and getting his bearings.

Pudditat didn't like other cats and acted like a bully around them. But he loved dogs. So he trotted right over to Terfel, Judy's chocolate Labrador mix, who was totally blind.

Judy had rescued Terfel, too. A neighbor she knew had become annoyed with the dog when he was just a puppy and had mistreated him. The abuse the puppy suffered destroyed his sight ... and his spirit. Judy opened her heart and home to the traumatized pup and named him after a famous Welsh singer.

Safe at last, Terfel grew into a good, gentle dog. But he couldn't see and often bumped into things and hurt himself. By the time Pudditat arrived, Terfel had also gone partly deaf. Afraid to go out, he rarely left his basket.

Perhaps Pudditat had suffered abuse himself. Or maybe it was that sixth sense again. Whatever the reason, Pudditat seemed to understand Terfel's problem. Before 24 hours had passed, the pushy, stray cat had connected with the timid, blind dog.

None of Judy's other cats had taken any special interest in their disabled housemate. Not so with Pudditat. Pudditat became Terfel's best friend, and always acted affectionate with the sweet-tempered dog. He hung out with Terfel all the time and rubbed his face against the dog's neck and legs. But that's not all.

*Pudditat rubs his body against the legs of his buddy, Terfel. Nobody knows for sure why cats do this, but it may be body language for, "I really like you."*

To Judy's amazement, Pudditat appointed himself Terfel's "seeing eye" cat. All on his own, Pudditat began coaxing the fearful dog out of his bed and leading him around the yard! And Terfel trusted him.

Then Judy got sick. Before entering the hospital, she brought her animals to Anne's cattery to be boarded. Not knowing how close they were, Anne housed them separately at first. But that changed after Anne called Judy to ask if she could take Terfel to a special church service for animals. "Yes," Judy said. "But you better bring Pudditat with him. He's Terfel's guide cat."

Guide cat? "I started to observe them more closely then," Anne says, "and their enormous bond was obvious."

From then on, Anne let the two animals outside together. She would let Pudditat out in the morning, and when she took Terfel for a walk later, she'd call "Pudditat," and the devoted feline would come running. Pudditat would take the lead, with Terfel close behind following his scent. Every so often, the cat would stop and nudge Terfel forward or wind around his legs to reassure him. "He gave Terfel confidence," Anne says. "Terfel would go farther with Pudditat along."

Unfortunately, Judy, who was in her 90s, died without ever becoming well enough to care for her animals again. So they stayed with Anne. In late 2015, Terfel, after living a long and rich rest of his life with Pudditat, also succumbed to old age.

"I miss seeing him and Pudditat cuddled together on the settee and nuzzling each other," Anne says. But she still has Pudditat. And now that Pudditat no longer has Terfel to look after, he cuddles with Anne instead. ●

Cats rule the Internet. A whopping two million cat videos were posted online in 2014 alone. That's 5,479 new videos every day, all year! Imagine how much time you could waste watching them, except ...

Scientists now think that watching cat videos is NOT a waste of time. It's actually good for us.

That's right. A 2012 Japanese study found that looking at images of cute animals improves viewers' concentration and ramps up job performance.

Jessica Gall Myrick, an Indiana University media researcher, in Bloomington, Indiana, U.S.A., also completed a study. She surveyed almost 7,000 cat video fans and discovered that watching adorable kitties gives people a break. It calms them down and cheers them up. Watchers get a burst of energy, which may make them better able to complete the task they were avoiding by watching videos in the first place.

So, if you find yourself *purr*-rusing video sites when you're supposed to be doing homework, it might be just what the doctor ordered.

# WHY WE LOVE CUTE CAT VIDEOS

# SALEM

🐾

## HOT ON THEIR TRAIL

*Domestic Shorthair/Kentucky, U.S.A.*

Salem the domestic house cat doesn't look as if he possesses any special powers. But he is all black. He was named after the Massachusetts, U.S.A., city famous for holding witch trials in the late 1600s. And he never meows; he howls like a dog. So, it might be best to keep an open mind.

Elizabeth Ober adopted Salem in 2004, when her husband was serving in the United States Air Force and stationed in Turkey. She got the cat from the animal shelter on the base. In the years following, Salem moved with them to Italy, Texas, and North Dakota, before landing in Lexington, Kentucky. But during their last move, from an apartment

> IT'S A MYTH THAT BLACK CATS HAVE A HARD TIME GETTING ADOPTED. THEY DON'T. IT'S JUST THAT THERE ARE MORE BLACK CATS THAN CATS OF ANY OTHER COLOR.

to a house eight miles (13 km) away, a skittish Salem bolted out their front door. "I saw a streak of black run across the living room floor," says Elizabeth. And her pet was gone.

Elizabeth stood outside and hollered for him, but Salem was afraid of the movers and didn't come. That was on November 1, 2014. Thinking he would come back when things settled down, Elizabeth put his bed, water, and a bowl of food on the porch of the apartment building. Every night, after she got off work, she drove back there to look for him and put out more food. "I could see little paw prints in the snow," Elizabeth says, "But I didn't know if it was him or another cat." Then, around Thanksgiving, the paw prints stopped coming and the food sat untouched.

Convinced that her kitty was gone forever, Elizabeth quit looking for him. But she still drove back to the old neighborhood five days a week to take her children, four-year-old Catherine and eight-year-old Jonathan, to day care and school. Both kids missed their couch kitty terribly. "Every day they asked, 'Is Salem coming back?'" says Elizabeth, who didn't know how to answer.

Two months later, Elizabeth drove home to see a black cat sitting on the sidewalk in front of their new house. "The kids went crazy," she says. "They kept hollering 'Salem, Salem. Salem has come home!'"

Elizabeth wasn't so sure. How could this skinny feline possibly be their cat? Salem didn't know where they lived. He had never once been to their new house. And to get there he had to cross two busy highways and hike through acres of farmland, in a trip that took 15 minutes by car. Then he had to pick the right house out of a huge subdivision.

*Impossible!* Elizabeth thought. She parked the car, and Jonathan jumped out calling Salem by name. Elizabeth lifted Catherine out of her car seat, while trying to hush Jonathan and calm his hopes. She was afraid if either of them tried to pick up the cat, he would get spooked and run away. So she took her kids up their front steps, unlocked the door, and went inside to get some cat food.

And that's when the cat walked up to them! He looked much too thin to be Salem, but then he did something only Salem would have done. He howled!

Lucky, the family's English cocker spaniel, greeted the cat like an old friend, licking him all over. And the cat trotted inside, like he owned the place.

Elizabeth was dumbfounded. The next day, she took the cat to her vet to have him scanned for a microchip, and the numbers matched!

"It was mind-blowing!" Elizabeth says. Many cats have been known to return to their home turf. But Salem went in search of his people. How he found them is difficult to explain.

Only one thing is for sure: "Salem likes us," says Catherine, which just goes to show that the power of love beats out witchcraft any day. ●

# Make your CAT feel at home

Like you, cats want their own "room." But unlike you, cats crave vertical space to climb, leap, and watch from above. Improving your cat's environment should make him happier and increase the bond between you. Here's how to start:

## FELINE FITNESS CENTER

You can make your own kitty gym, which is nothing more than a souped-up scratching post. Start by finding a bark-covered, fallen tree branch that is dry, free of bugs, three to four inches (7.6–10.2 cm) in diameter, and four to five feet (1.2–1.5 m) high. Ask an adult to help you saw off one end, at an angle, so the log will sit flat on the floor when you prop it in a corner. Hang a cat toy from the top, rub the branch with catnip, or wind some sisal rope around the middle third. Then watch your kitty work out.

### ROOM WITH A VIEW

Who wants to stay inside staring at four walls? Certainly not your curious kitty. Give her a window seat by placing a pillow on a windowsill, where she can sit and keep tabs on the neighborhood. If you don't have a ledge wide enough for that, drag an overstuffed chair in front of a window so your cat can perch on the back.

### SAFE HAVEN

A scaredy-cat needs somewhere to run. What could be better than a safe, secure spot from which she can look down on every-one else? The Internet is full of ideas for building catwalks using ramps, shelves, and narrow, wall-mounted steps. But the simplest solution is to put a cat bed on the top shelf of a cupboard or bookcase and arrange the furniture so your cat can reach it.

### ALONE TIME

Do you have a secret place? Kitties need a place to retreat to when they're scared or tired. And it doesn't need to be expensive—just dark and snug feeling. Putting a towel over a cat carrier and leaving the door open works great. Or you can make your own kitty hideaway out of a cardboard box lined with soft cloth. Cut a doorway in one side and a little "window" high up on another. Now Snuggles can safely settle in at home.

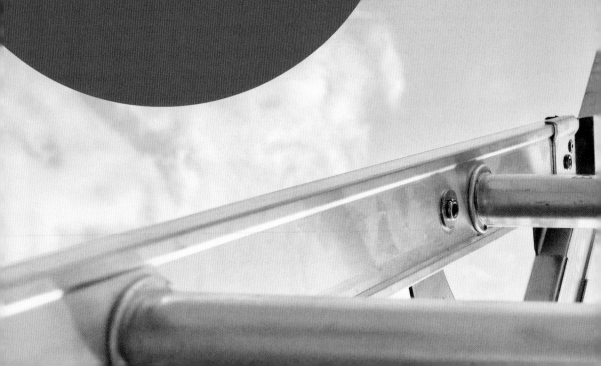

ADVENTUROUS

# DODGER

## FRIENDLY RIDER

*Domestic Shorthair/England, United Kingdom*

Dodger the ginger tabby waited his turn like everyone else. Lying on a wooden bench inside the glass-enclosed bus shelter in Bridport, Dorset, England, he waited for his ride to appear. That would be city bus number X53. When it hissed to a stop, Dodger hopped off his bench and sat on the sidewalk beside the bus. There he stayed, calmly scratching his neck with his hind leg, while the human passengers disembarked. Once they were off, everyone waiting to board formed a line.

It went like this: A man carrying a yellow shopping bag got on first. Next was a lady wearing a purple jacket. Then came Dodger followed

SCIENTISTS THINK CATS RIDE PUBLIC TRANSPORTATION FOR THREE REASONS: THEY ARE USED TO PEOPLE, PEOPLE ARE MOST LIKELY FEEDING THEM, AND BUSES MAKE CATS FEEL WARM AND SAFE.

by a smiling, middle-aged woman. The double doors slid closed, and Dodger strolled down the center aisle looking for a seat. People couldn't help but chuckle; the cheeky kitty knew the routine so well.

"Dodger was a moody fellow," says Fee Jeanes, who adopted him as a kitten. "But he just loved being around people." She named the friendly feline after the character in *Oliver Twist*, a classic novel by Charles Dickens. As a young cat, Dodger spent his nights curled up on the foot of Fee's bed and his days stretched out on the sofa back. It wasn't until his family moved next door to the bus station that the furry homebody took to the road.

"He still ate all his meals at home," Fee says, "and he always came home to go to bed." But one day, her teenage daughter Emily called her with upsetting news. One of Emily's friends had spotted Dodger prowling around Chideock, another town about a ten-minute drive from home. She sent Emily a video of the traveling cat. "You have to go get him!" Emily told her mother.

*An intrepid Dodger relaxes in the arms of his owner, Fee Jeanes, after a day on the road. Fee allowed her cat to roam as far as he pleased, so long as he returned home for supper.*

Her heart pounding, Fee hopped in her car and rushed to the bus station. But as soon as she got there, a bus pulled up. Swish. Its doors opened, and Dodger ambled off!

Fee stood there openmouthed, while her cat just looked at her. "I'm coming home, Mum," he seemed to say. "Don't worry about me."

But Fee did worry. What if her happy wanderer got on one of the coaches bound for Cornwall? Cornwall was three hours away. Fee figured Dodger would never get back

*What, me hurry? Not Dodger. This ginger tabby hangs around while human passengers hustle aboard the waiting bus. But not to worry. Frequent rider Dodger will climb on in time.*

from there. So she hung around to see what happened next.

And, just as she had feared, Dodger soon boarded another bus. Fee hurried to warn the driver, only to have the driver say she knew all about her furry hitchhiker. Dodger was a regular on her route. What's more, her other passengers loved him. One fellow brought Dodger a yummy snack of cooked cod, and a bowl to eat it from, every day.

The local paper picked up Dodger's story. Before long, he had fans as far away as Australia. People were sending him toys and treats and coming to Bridport just to see him. Others called the number printed on Dodger's collar. "Have you lost your cat?" they would ask.

"I'd say, 'no,'" says Fee. "'He's fine, and he knows what he's doing.'"

*Watching carefully from the wooden bench inside the bus shelter in Bridport, Dodger waits for the bus to arrive, right on schedule.*

But one woman shared a touching story. She said she suffered from cancer, and she so looked forward to seeing Dodger on her bus trips to the hospital for chemotherapy. The gentle cat comforted her by sitting on her lap and purring.

By the time Dodger died in 2012, at the ripe old age of 16, he had logged thousands of miles. But this well-traveled cat, who became famous for riding the bus, did not like riding in cars. "I only took him a few times," Fee says. "But when I did, he sat on the seat and growled. He just hated it." ●

# KULI

## MAKING WAVES

*Domestic Shorthair/Hawaii, U.S.A.*

Surf's up! Alex Gomez, of Honolulu, Hawaii, grabs her board and runs toward the rolling breakers. Close on her heels is Kuli, her one-eyed white-and-yellow cat. Alex is holding his leash. She slaps her surfboard down on the water and sits on the back of it, while the fluffy-tailed feline climbs up on the front. And *cat-abunga!* He lies down right on the nose of the board, with his paws hanging ten. Granted the waves are small, only knee-high or lower. Still, the woman and her cat ride one wave after another, enjoying the sport and each other's company. They've been surfing together since 2015, and it never gets old.

KULI THE CAT ISN'T THE ONLY ANIMAL THAT SURFS. DOGS, PIGS, GOATS, ALPACAS, AND EVEN MICE HAVE BEEN KNOWN TO RIDE THE WAVES.

When Alex and her roommate, Krista Littleton, decided to get a pet, they wanted one they could take on outdoor adventures. Also, being special education teachers, they wanted an animal with special needs. And whatever pet they chose had to be okay left alone at home for stretches, because they both work long hours.

So what did they get? A tiny, one-pound (0.5-kg) kitten that had lost one eye due to an infection! The women adopted the furry handful from an animal shelter and immediately named him Nanakuli, after a lovely Hawaiian valley. According to legend, Nanakuli has several meanings, including "to look blind or deaf." Kuli wasn't blind. He could see out of his remaining eye. But Krista says, "He was such a bag of bones that you could feel every bump in his spine."

When she and Alex first brought him home, the kitty gobbled up everything in sight. But no matter what he ate, he couldn't keep the food down. He threw up so often that he needed baths twice a day to keep his fur clean. For about a month, Kuli was so sick that the women feared he wouldn't survive. Then, suddenly, he rallied and began gaining weight. And as for all those baths? Alex and Krista now believe they helped the three of them bond, and taught Kuli to tolerate water. "He trusts us," Alex says, "and thinks anything we do is okay."

But would his trust extend to surfboarding? That was asking a lot. Still, the two teachers wanted to give it a shot. They started by bringing Kuli to a quiet beach, where the water was calm. Then they set his cat carrier on the sand and propped open the door. "We stayed near him," says Krista. "But we allowed him to come in and out of the carrier as he wanted."

Next, Alex put her surfboard in the water and let Kuli sit on it. Standing beside him, she gently splashed water on his paws. Another training exercise involved him sitting on

*Honolulu's skyscrapers shimmer in the distance, but an already wet Kuli stares straight ahead as he speeds toward the shore at Waikiki Beach.*

the board while she walked alongside it, from one end to the other. Especially important was teaching Kuli to swim, first with a life jacket and then without.

She wanted him to know to swim back to the board, in case he ever fell off. "Baby steps made all this possible," Alex says. "We exposed him to a little bit at a time." Training took practice and patience ... and lots of time.

But one day, he got it! "I was so excited," says Krista.

Today, Kuli is known as the surfing cat. There are videos of him online, and he has a growing following on social media. He rarely needs his life jacket anymore and even has his own foam surfboard that lets him dig in his claws so he feels secure.

"We can tell he likes it," Alex says. "Because when we open our beach bag, he purrs and jumps right in." No doubt about it. Kuli the water-loving cat is one cool, surfer dude! ●

## ASK AN **EXPERT**

**Q:** Why do humans find cats so mysterious?

**DR. WEITZMAN:** We can't figure them out. Seriously, this is true. Take the cat who all of a sudden goes tearing across the living room for no apparent reason. Or the cuddly cat who's loving you and then reaches over and swats you for petting her too long. Cats will always keep us guessing.

*Kuli enjoys the water on a bright Hawaiian summer day. Keeping Kuli on a leash lets Alex grab him quickly, if necessary.*

# DIDGA

## TOP PERFORMER

*Domestic Shorthair/New South Wales, Australia*

How do you pick a talented cat—one that will be easy to train? Robert Dollwet, a longtime Hollywood animal trainer who had recently moved to New South Wales, Australia, knew what to do. But even he got off to a false start when he went to an animal shelter searching for one. He started out wanting a boy cat. "I thought boys would have more gusto," he says.

But he soon discovered a playful female kitten who was creating all kinds of commotion. "I never get an animal based on looks," Robert says. Character and temperament matter most to him. So he clapped his hands and waved his hat in the air to see what she would do.

( TO BUILD A CAT'S CONFIDENCE, EXPOSE HER
TO NEW SIGHTS, SOUNDS, AND SMELLS
BY TAKING HER DIFFERENT PLACES AS A KITTEN.
KEEP HER IN A CARRIER AT FIRST.
LATER, YOU CAN WALK HER ON A LEASH. )

"She acted confident and unfazed," Robert says. "And she had a lot of energy."
*Purr*-fect!

Robert adopted the 13-week-old ball of fluff and named her Didga, short for didger-idoo, an Australian musical instrument Robert was learning to play. When he began teaching Didga, he used mealtime as training time. He would hold a meaty tidbit out to her and urge her to step forward, jump up, step back, and more, with his voice.

When she did what he wanted, he clicked a "clicker" and fed her the food. Once she mastered clicker training, Robert taught Didga where to go on cue using a target stick and how to do basic tricks. Within a few months, Didga was jumping up into his hands and walking on a leash.

Wanting to keep her safe, he never let Didga roam free. Instead, he used training to stimulate her mind. By 2015, she had mastered so many tricks that she set a Guinness World Record for performing the most tricks by a cat in one minute. That required she first learn 24 individual tricks like high-five, shake, roll over, and spin. Then she learned to

*Didga poses like a statue on the outstretched hand of her owner and trainer,
Robert Dollwet. It's a tricky balancing act,
but Robert never forces Didga to do anything that frightens her.*

*Didga exudes self-confidence as she cruises through the park on her skateboard.*

do them all, in quick succession, before earning a treat. Pretty good, huh?

Yes. But that is not her star trick. That would be skateboarding. And that was Didga's own idea! That's right. Didga was still a kitten when Robert took her into town walking on the leash and they stopped at an outdoor juice bar. Another patron had left his skateboard on the ground while buying a drink. And Didga spotted it. Instead of steering clear, she walked right over ... and stepped right onto it!

Robert hurried home, dug out an old skateboard of his own, and discovered she was a natural. How natural?

One day, Robert was walking in his house, when the sound of clattering wheels caught his attention. What did he see but Didga sitting on the board and rolling past him! "I couldn't stop laughing," he says.

The funny sight inspired Robert to combine cat training, gravity, and some trick photography to produce a series of online videos. Set to music, they appear to show Didga zipping up and down ramps, shredding half pipes, and jumping obstacles at a skateboard park. One video even shows the furry athlete doing a "hippy jump" over the back of a friendly Rottweiler and coming down on her moving board. She is so sure of herself that once, when she slipped off her board, the feline skater didn't bat a paw. She simply ran and hopped right back on—without so much as a word from her coach. How's that for star quality?

A lap cat Didga is not. "She'll come over for an occasional rub," says Robert. But cuddling is not her thing. This is one cat who prefers the skateboard park to a comfy bed by the fire. And her millions of fans are happy that she does. ●

*The freewheeling Didga rolls by a classic car on display during the annual 1950s and 1960s nostalgia festival called Cooly Rocks On, in Coolangatta, Queensland, Australia.*

# MILLIE

## KITTY ROCK STAR

*Domestic Shorthair/Utah, U.S.A.*

No wonder people stopped and stared. A man was hauling himself up a sheer rock wall by his fingertips—with a cat strapped to his shoulders! "We must have looked ridiculous," says Craig Armstrong, of Salt Lake City, Utah.

Craig is an experienced climber. He has scaled boulders and craggy cliffs alone and with friends. But on many trips, he saw other climbers who had brought along their dogs. That started him day-dreaming. "I knew someday I would take a pet with me," Craig says, "Only it would be a cat, because cats are super cute." But how do you get a nervous kitty to enjoy rock climbing and still keep her safe?

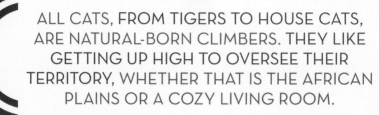

ALL CATS, FROM TIGERS TO HOUSE CATS, ARE NATURAL-BORN CLIMBERS. THEY LIKE GETTING UP HIGH TO OVERSEE THEIR TERRITORY, WHETHER THAT IS THE AFRICAN PLAINS OR A COZY LIVING ROOM.

Millie was only two months old when Craig started taking her to a local park that had a pond with an island in it. There, he let her run free.

Then, once she got used to being outside, he changed their outings to Stansbury Island, a huge island in the Great Salt Lake. Stansbury was dry and barren, like the desert landscape where Craig eventually wanted to take Millie rock climbing. "On Stansbury, I would start hiking up a hill," Craig says, "and she would follow. No way did she want to be left out there all alone." That's how he got Millie used to scampering after him and thinking of him as her safe place.

Finally, Millie was ready. Craig bought her a harness that he reinforced with rope and took her to a giant wall of rock called 1,000 Feet of Fun. But cats are independent creatures. Unlike dogs, who work in packs, cats hunt alone. Being strapped to Craig and carried up cliffs made Millie anxious. She seemed to want to climb under her own power and do it her own way.

So Craig tried attaching Millie to his own harness with a long cord, but letting her

*A tired Millie rides on Craig's shoulder, beside his crash pad,*
*which he lays at the foot of each boulder they climb, to cushion falls.*

*Millie leads Craig on a glorious, five-mile (8-km)-long "catting" expedition through Little Wild Horse Canyon in San Rafael Swell, Utah.*

free-climb. Free climbing is rock climbing using only your feet and hands—or in Millie's case, all four paws—to grip the rock surface. Craig used ropes to protect her and himself from falling, but not to help pull themselves up. However, after a few such trips, Craig realized something was still wrong.

Millie didn't like it! "I had spent so many hours with her that I could tell she was stressed," Craig says. Her tail was puffy and stiff. She meowed a lot, and her whole body looked tense.

As a responsible pet owner, Craig had two choices. He could leave his little buddy at home, or he could change the way he climbed. Zac Robinson, Craig's longtime climbing partner, also had a cat. So the two men agreed on a radical approach. On Friday nights, they drove to their rock climbing destination and slept in tents or the back of Craig's pickup truck. On Saturdays, they and their cats would complete an easy free climb, maybe down into a beautiful rocky canyon. The secret was letting the cats lead, which meant moving slower and going in unexpected directions. "Where we would have taken a straight route," Craig explains, "the cats followed a natural line, like falling water."

On Sundays, the men let their carefully trained cats loose in the desert. Then the men wandered around after the furry little lizard chasers and experienced nature from their animals' point of view. Zac dubbed the activity "catting."

"We saw things we would have walked right past before," Craig says. "It was super fun." All this makes for some unique experiences. But does it mean Millie herself is highly unusual? "No," says Craig. "She's just a funny little house cat." A funny little house cat that gets to share his adventure-filled life. ●

## ASK AN **EXPERT**

**Q:** What can people do to help their precious cats live longer, healthier lives?

**DR. WEITZMAN:** Keep them behaviorally enriched. That means giving your cat things to do and choices to make. Outdoor cats face so many dangers that we now often keep these avid prowlers and explorers confined 24 hours a day. Indoor cats, while safe from the outside world, can't help getting bored and stressed. So, scatter Missy's kibble and make her search for it, or put a cat flap in a closet door so Wilbur can hide when he wants to. Enrichment takes work, but it's vital for cat health.

# MANNY

✿

## LIVING THE HIGH LIFE

*Domestic Shorthair/New York City, U.S.A.*

On July 22, 2015, a homeless black cat found himself in terrible trouble. He was stuck more than 30 stories above the East River, on New York City's Manhattan Bridge. "He was a rack of bones and so desperate for food that he went up there chasing a pigeon," says Lisa Hara Levin, a veterinarian and medical director of Animal Care Centers of New York City.

The Manhattan Bridge is a jam-packed, more than 100-year-old suspension bridge that connects Manhattan and Brooklyn. About 450,000 commuters zip across its double-decker roadway every weekday. But none of them could see the unlucky kitty—who

> A CAT'S CLAWS ARE CURVED INWARD
> AND DIG IN WHEN CLIMBING UPWARD.
> BUT INWARD-CURVING CLAWS DON'T HELP
> WHEN COMING DOWN, WHICH IS WHY
> SOME CATS GET STUCK UP IN TREES.

was trapped on a narrow stone ledge—pacing back and forth.

It was office workers peering out skyscraper windows who spotted his predicament. One of them called the Animal Care Centers, which then asked the city's Department of Transportation (DOT) for help. With cars, trucks, and subway trains zooming by all around them, caring workmen devised a plan. For safety's sake, DOT ironworkers first closed one lane of traffic on the lower level of the bridge. Then Kevin Sexton, a field supervisor for the Animal Care Centers, baited a wire box trap with cat food. He set the trap on a maintenance platform attached to one of the bridge's giant support columns, and hoped the hungry kitty would come to eat. But he didn't.

So Kevin bravely swallowed his own fear of heights and crawled toward the little creature to lure him closer. That worked. The cat entered the trap, and Kevin lifted it to a waiting helper. Then he drove to the Animal Care Centers' emergency clinic, where a vet examined the cat for injuries. "The poor fellow looked pretty bad," says Dr. Levin. "One eye was destroyed. One of his hind legs was ripped open. And he had an old wound on his tail."

Of all his injuries, the damage to his eye was the most serious. Most likely, it had been poked during one of the hapless hunter's run-ins with a pigeon. If infection set in, the germs could shoot from his eye through his optic nerve and straight to the kitty's brain. If that happened, it would kill him.

So the vet went to work. After pumping the frightened cat full of painkillers, she cleaned his wounds and gave him antibiotics. Then she scheduled surgery to remove his ruined eye, amputate the decaying part of his tail, and stitch up the gash in his leg. She also had him neutered, so he wouldn't father any kittens and add to the city's already large population of street cats.

Not so long ago, any friendless cat taken to an animal shelter and in need of so much expensive medical care would have been humanely euthanized. But that changed in 2003. That's when the Mayor's Alliance for NYC's Animals was formed. This union of more than 150 nonprofit animal shelters and rescue groups works together to end euthanasia and help unwanted animals find forever homes. Today, they save more than eight out of ten of the animals that are turned in to them.

The Manhattan Bridge cat, since named Manny, proved to be one of their biggest success stories. Despite undergoing multiple surgeries and suffering several serious setbacks during his four-month-long recovery, Manny is healthy again. Sure, he's missing an eye, and his tail is shorter than it used to be. But the feisty feline feels good enough to race around his foster home like a miniature torpedo, jumping on bookshelves and knocking over plants. Dr. Levin is thrilled by his transformation. "Whenever I think of Manny," she says, "I thank God he ended up with us." ●

# FELINE
## WALKABOUTS
### Teach your cat to walk on a leash

Surfboarding. Rock climbing. Skateboarding. Even a walk in the park. Every kind of outdoor adventuring presents risk for your cat. For this reason, your cat must be trained to walk on a leash. That's the best way to keep him safe. And you can train him yourself! Here's how:

### BUY A CLICKER AT A PET STORE

A clicker is a cheap little noisemaker used as a training tool. At the instant your cat does what you want, you click the clicker. Then, immediately after clicking, you reward your cat. The routine goes like this: Command, click, reward. Cats are smart and will catch on. Repeat these steps ten minutes a day, every day, for two weeks, and your cat will learn to associate the command with the reward. But you must keep your cool, and give him time.

94

## HARNESS TRAINING

Ply your kitty with treats while putting on his harness. Adjust the harness so it fits snugly, but isn't too tight, and distract your cat with playing or petting. Let him wear the harness while he eats, and feed him only his favorite fresh meat.

## LEASH TRAINING

When your cat accepts the harness, attach a very lightweight leash. Do not pull on the leash. Just hold the leash loosely. Once he is used to the leash, urge him to walk. Here's how:

**1.** Hold the leash in one hand and a treat in the other. Take two steps forward, and call your kitty by name. Be patient, and don't tug. When your furry friend walks toward the treat, click and give it to him.

**2.** Repeat this over and over, gradually making your cat take more steps before earning his reward.

**3.** At the end of every training session, tell your cat to sit. When he does, click and reward him.

**4.** Gradually walk faster and add turns. Remember to use only your voice to tell kitty what to do, without pulling on the leash.

## WALKING OUTDOORS

Now that your cat is used to the harness and leash and will walk beside you, take him outside. The big outdoors contains many distractions, which will compete for your cat's attention. So, if possible, start in a safe, quiet place, like a fenced-in public tennis court. Later, you and your kitty can enjoy the challenge of exploring new and different places.

HARDWORKING

# SABLE

## FELINE CROSSING GUARD

*Domestic Shorthair/Washington, U.S.A.*

Can cats tell time? Sable, an elderly, black, domestic shorthair, apparently could. Every weekday morning and again in the afternoon, he would trot out from his family's garage and go to work. His job was right across the street, at Enterprise Middle School, in West Richland, Washington. Sable was a volunteer crossing guard. He helped make sure the school's students, ages 11 and 12, made it safely across the busy street.

No one told Sable to do this. It was his own idea, maybe born of age. As a young cat, Sable lived on the streets. He simply showed up in Tamara and Lance Morrison's backyard one day and stayed. But it

**BLACK CATS MAKE DEVOTED PETS.** BUT EVIDENCE SUGGESTS THEY MAY PROVE UNLUCKY FOR ALLERGY SUFFERERS. **SCIENTISTS SUGGEST THAT THESE OWNERS KEEP DARK-COLORED CATS** OUT OF THEIR BEDROOMS.

wasn't until years later, after the Morrisons moved to West Richland, that he adopted his crosswalk duties. "He just came down the driveway and sat by one of our safety patrol kids," says Monti Franckowiak, Enterprise's safety patrol director. She wasn't too surprised, at first. But then Sable kept coming. "That cat was like clockwork," she says. "He never missed a day."

As Monti scanned the traffic and watched the kids, so did Sable. "He and I made a lot of eye contact," she says. "He was always looking around and checking to see that the safety patrol kids were doing their job."

In two years of working together, Monti never picked up the cat. He rubbed against her legs, and she bent down and petted him. But theirs was not a sentimental relationship. Monti and Sable behaved like colleagues doing the same job. "It seemed like the cat was there to work," Monti says. "It really did."

Street-smart Sable seemed to know better than to run into traffic. He always sat on his own side of the road, usually on the sidewalk right by the safety patrol's station.

And there he stayed, unless a student needed him ...

One cold, winter day, a slick coating of ice covered the road and sidewalks. Monti saw a boy step off the curb, on the far side of the street, and lose his footing. *Wham!* Down he fell, flat on his back. Monti headed over to help, but she had to pick her way to avoid falling herself. Not to worry. "Sable got to him before I could," Monti says. "The cat was rubbing against him, licking his face by his ear, and sniffing. 'Don't worry,' Sable seemed to say. 'I took care of him.'"

The "crossing guard cat" was so lovable and dependable that the school made him an honorary member of the safety patrol. Monti had an official certificate printed up, and she and a crew of seven kids presented it to Sable's owner. His owner, in turn, bought Sable his very own safety vest and began putting it on him every morning before he went out.

What a sight the safety patrol made—seven kids, one adult, and one cat all standing in their assigned spots and all wearing neon green and bright orange vests. No wonder drivers slowed their cars and took pictures. "I looked forward to seeing that cat every day," Monti says. "So did the kids. 'Hurry up,' they'd say. 'Sable will be waiting.'"

During summer vacation 2013, Sable retired. Eighteen years old by then, he may have decided it was time to lie back and take life easy. Monti and the schoolkids miss him. But Sable taught everyone who loved him the importance of being reliable and caring for others. And far from bringing anybody bad luck, this all-black feline brought only extreme good fortune. Not one child was ever injured crossing the street when that cat was in charge. ●

# BAGEL

## FLASHY FELINE FUND-RAISER
### *Domestic Shorthair/California, U.S.A.*

People gasp in surprise when they first see Bagel. "Wow!" they exclaim. "It's a cat!" Then they laugh. Many assume a cat wearing blinged-out sunglasses is a Hollywood thing. After all, Bagel and her owner, Karen McGill, do live in Los Angeles, California. And Los Angeles is home to Hollywood—a famous, moviemaking neighborhood that oozes glamour and glitz.

But Bagel doesn't wear sunglasses to look cool. She's a cross-eyed, special needs cat. The fancy-looking specs actually serve as protective goggles. Bagel can see. But she was born with eyelid agenesis. Her upper eyelids are missing, and she can't make tears. This means she

**CATS HAVE THREE EYELIDS—AN UPPER, A LOWER, AND ONE CALLED THE NICTITATING MEMBRANE. THAT THIRD EYELID SWEEPS ACROSS THE EYEBALL LIKE A WINDSHIELD WIPER, HELPING TO WHISK AWAY DEBRIS.**

can't blink to protect her eyes from debris. Then, once dirt or grime blows into them, she has no tears to wash it out. So Karen dreamed up the protective sunglasses idea and ordered a custom-made pair. She glued on crystals to make them a lot more fun.

Naturally, Bagel pawed off her eyewear at first. But she soon adjusted. "What a great idea!" said Bagel's vet, when she saw Bagel wearing her shades.

But sunglasses can't fix everything. Unfortunately, even though Bagel lacks eyelids, she still has eyelashes. They grow in the corners of her eyes and scratch her corneas. Three operations to prevent the eyelashes from growing back failed. So Karen applies eyedrops to Bagel's eyes every day and tweezes out the painful lashes once a week.

And Bagel never objects! "I put her on her back," says Karen. "And she wraps her paws around my arm and lets me do it. She's very uncatlike."

That's for sure. Bagel doesn't meow. She can't climb trees. And, rather than being carried, the trusting feline insists on sitting upright on Karen's hand, "like a long-tailed Buddha."

*Bagel, a born model, poses at the Public Art Walls in Venice Beach, California. Karen often takes her there for walks.*

*Whether Bagel wears dog clothes (shown here), baby clothes, or an outfit handmade for her, this well-dressed kitty always looks like a glamour puss.*

Besides her eye problem, Bagel suffers from allergies and an inability to adjust to changes in air temperature. One day, Karen was walking her on the beach, when the cat started shivering. *Whaaat?* Karen wasn't cold, and Bagel was covered in fur. But Karen rushed to the pet store and bought her a cozy sweatshirt. Then Bagel was fine. She now wears warm clothes most days, and sports a supermodel wardrobe of everything from coats and sweaters to capes and ball gowns.

Karen didn't know about Bagel's health issues before she adopted her. And soon after, money troubles forced Karen into homelessness. For two months, Karen lived in her car. Yet she continued caring for Bagel and took her everywhere she went. Strangers helped pay for Bagel's surgeries, and Karen eventually got a better job. No longer homeless, she says those difficult days deepened Bagel's bond with her.

Now the "Sunglass Cat" is leading the way. She was invited to enter a national contest for America's next cat superstar. Even though Bagel lost the title, she won the popular vote. Since then, Karen and Bagel have appeared on TV, and Bagel even stylishly walked the red carpet at New York City's Couture Fashion Week.

In addition, they've done countless "meet and greet" fund-raisers for charity. Above all, Karen wants to show others that special needs cats have much to offer. She hopes to inspire more people to adopt them. But the best encounter, the one that won Karen's heart, happened by chance.

She was carrying Bagel on the beach when they met a father and his 12-year-old daughter. The daughter was in a wheelchair and was unable to speak. But Bagel seemed to sense something in her. For the first time, Bagel jumped off Karen's hand. She landed on the girl's chest, circled once, and snuggled down—gazing into her eyes. "Her dad was overwhelmed," Karen says. "And to see that little girl smile is what it's all about. It made me feel so good ... if people can relate to Bagel, it makes it easier for them to deal with life." ●

## ASK AN **EXPERT**

**Q:** What special skills or unique attributes do cats possess?

**DR. WEITZMAN:** They are physical marvels, with a height-ened sense of touch (think whiskers), vision (especially night vision), hearing, and smell. Add to that their superior agility, speed, and grace, and a remarkable ability to squeeze through small spaces. Our snuggly pets are like little superheroes in disguise.

# HUMPHREY

## OFFICIAL GOVERNMENT MOUSER

*Domestic Longhair/England, United Kingdom*

Something had to be done. Mice and rats had taken over No. 10 Downing Street, London, the official home of Britain's prime minister. So, in 1989, when a government employee found a one-year-old black-and-white stray cat roaming about, he nabbed the kitty for the prime minister's residence. The cat was christened Humphrey, after a popular character on a British television show. The government agreed to pay for his keep, and the new mouser moved in.

When not hunting rodents, Humphrey spent most of his time curled up on the doorkeeper's chair. Visitors warmed to the friendly feline, who added a homey touch to the fancy place. Or so he did until 1994.

That year Prime Minister John Major was in power, and elections were coming up. Wanting publicity, Mr. Major called the *Daily Telegraph*'s political editor, George Jones, requesting an interview. Jones and a photographer hurried to oblige. They arrived at the prime minister's residence, only to find Mr. Major excited about a family of robins nesting in a window box outside his office. The two men followed Mr. Major out on the terrace to see the birds. But what did they find? The lifeless bodies of four baby robins! For some unknown reason, their mother had abandoned the nest.

And matters got worse!

Instead of sticking to the facts, like reporters should, George Jones made up a story. "Who killed cock (or hen) robin?" he asked, then suggested, "Humphrey, the Downing Street cat is under suspicion."

Readers gasped in horror. So many complaints bombarded the prime minister's office that the government issued a press release. "Humphrey has been ill with kidney trouble," read the statement. "He could not have caught anything, even if it had been roast duck with orange sauce presented to him on a plate."

The prime minister himself declared, "Humphrey has been unjustly accused ... Humphrey is not a serial killer."

But the damage had been done. Outrage over the scandal continued. Perhaps Humphrey was not "ameowsed," because he disappeared soon after.

When three months had passed with no sign of the cat, the *Times* reported that Humphrey had died. Alongside his obituary, they printed his picture. Good thing, because medics at a nearby hospital saw it. Lo and behold, the supposedly "stray" cat they had adopted and named PC (Patrol Cat) was none other than Humphrey.

*Humphrey strolls outside his famous residence in London, England.*

*When rumors swirled that Humphrey had died, photographers proved them false by posing the cat with the daily paper.*

The prime minister's office was notified and sent a car to collect the wandering feline. News that Humphrey had been found flew around the world. Socks, a cat belonging to United States president Bill Clinton, even sent a note of congratulations.

But another scandal soon erupted. On May 1, 1997, the British elected a new prime minister. Within six months of him moving into No. 10 Downing Street, Humphrey was gone. Kicked out, the losing party said. Rumors claimed that the prime minister's wife hated cats and she had Humphrey put to sleep.

The truth was that Humphrey's kidney trouble had gotten worse, and he was retired for medical reasons. A government worker who wished to remain anonymous took the cat to live with him. But, given Humphrey's scandalous history, people refused to believe it. The uproar grew so intense that photographers were called. Sworn to secrecy, they took pictures of Humphrey sitting on top of the daily paper, to prove he survived.

The controversial cat lived to be 18 years old and passed away peacefully on March 20, 2006. The next day, editor George Jones finally fessed up and cleared Humphrey's name. "Humphrey deserves a posthumous pardon," he wrote in his newspaper column. Thus ended the life and career of Britain's most famous political scapegoat, or should we say, scapecat. ●

Want a meowing good time? Scoot on over to a cat café! A cat café is a place where animal lovers hang out. While there, they drink coffee, eat cat-shaped cookies, and play with friendly felines. The cafés first appeared in Taiwan and Japan. In those countries, many people live in crowded apartment buildings that don't allow pets.

America's first known cat café popped up in 2014 in New York City. It was only open for four days, but hundreds of feline fanatics stood in line for hours to get inside. Once admitted, they could cuddle up with 16 cute kitties, who batted at feather toys, lazed in the windows, or nuzzled customers' legs. Since then, several purr-manent, copycat cafés have sprung up around the country. Others can be found in Paris, France, and London, England.

The best thing about them, besides giving cat lovers their kitty "fix," is that most café cats come from animal shelters. They're available for adoption, and many café customers have gone home bearing a new fur-ever friend.

# CAT CAFÉS

# NUDGE

## FOUR-LEGGED FIRE LOOKOUT

*Maine Coon/New York State, U.S.A.*

The stray cat had been showing up for weeks. Dominic "Nic" Pascal, of Jamesville, New York, U.S.A., would see it sitting in the path he mows through his 30-acre (12-ha) woods. "Someone probably drove by and dumped her," Nic says. "Every time I went to get her, she would run." But he started setting food out and waited.

Finally, one day, she let him scoop her up and take her to the vet. After checking her teeth, the vet guessed the fluffy kitty to be between 18 and 24 months old. But then he said when cats get stuck outdoors without food, they often chew the bark off trees. "Have a look," he said, opening the cat's mouth again. Her top front teeth were worn down to nubs!

## SCIENTISTS DIDN'T KNOW HOW TO MAKE COMMERCIAL CAT FOOD THAT SATISFIES ALL OF A CAT'S NUTRITIONAL NEEDS UNTIL THE LATE 1980s.

Weeks passed. Whenever Nic put the cat on the couch and tried to play with her, she lowered her head and bumped him like a bull. Her head-butting, combined with the fact that her arrival gave Nic the "nudge" he needed to adopt a cat, led Nic's wife, Kathy, to christen the newcomer. "Let's call her 'Nudge,'" she suggested. And the name stuck.

Since the Pascals live out in the country and Nudge liked going outside, Nic installed a cat flap in their bedroom window. "She's in and out all the time," says Nic.

Before long, she began bringing him presents—live presents of moles, mice, chipmunks, and birds. Thank you gifts, perhaps? Nudge usually delivered one a week, which Nic would catch and release outside.

Once, he woke up to find Nudge staring into the dark space behind their entertainment center. With the help of a flashlight and a pair of long-handled grippers, Nic pulled out a motionless brown lump. "It was a ferret," he says. "And I thought she'd killed it." But she hadn't. The minute Nic opened the back door, the ferret sprang to life and ran.

Then came the morning of April 9, 2010, which began like any other. Nic got up at

6 a.m. and fed the cat. "Come back in when you're ready," Nic said, as he let her out into his attached garage. The garage door was open, so she could go outside. Then Nic went back to bed and back to sleep.

About an hour later, the usually silent Nudge jumped on his chest and warbled at him. "Go away. We want more sleep," Nic mumbled, as he gently pushed her onto the floor. But Nudge did not go away. She jumped on his chest again, this time with her claws out. "Ouch!" yelled Nic. "What is the matter with you?" Annoyed, he got up and walked into the hall. And that's when he saw it. Black smoke was billowing out of the garage and into the house!

"Kathy! Get up," he screamed and dialed 911.

Firefighters arrived and extinguished the blaze, but not before flames had destroyed Nic's three classic convertibles, all his tools, and gardening supplies. Had Nudge not warned him, who knows what would have happened?

Some people might say she only woke Nic so he would save her, by opening a door. But Nudge didn't need rescuing. She was already outside. Instead of staying outdoors she came back in the house through her cat flap. There could be only one possible reason. She wanted to save her people. "Your cat came in and got you!" said the fire chief, shaking his head in amazement. "I'd keep that cat!"

The American Red Cross of Central New York was equally impressed. On December 1, at their 12th Annual Real Heroes Breakfast, they awarded Nudge their Hero of the Year award. Fifteen hundred people clapped and cheered for the first cat ever to receive it. ●

# TAMA

## RAILWAY STATIONMASTER
*Domestic Shorthair/Kinokawa, Japan*

Tama was a very fine pet cat. She was born in the shop next door to Kishi train station, in the rural Japanese neighborhood of Kinokawa. Kinokawa lay 8.7 miles (14 km) outside of Wakayama City. Residents depended on the train to travel between the two places. Tama's owner let her cat visit the station and its travelers during the day, and even installed a little cat house inside the station.

But the privately owned railway was losing money and planned to shut down. People would have to find another way to go to the city. And Tama's owner had to remove her cat house.

CALICO CATS HAVE RED-AND-BLACK COATS **WITH DISTINCT PATCHES OF WHITE,** USUALLY ON THE UNDERSIDE OF THEIR BODIES. THESE TRICOLORED KITTIES ARE ALMOST ALWAYS FEMALE.

Fortunately, the Wakayama Electric Railway Company bought the struggling railway line and kept the trains running. But what about Tama? "The cat's owner adored the cat like a child," says Ms. Keiko Yamaki, spokesperson for the railway company. So Tama's owner boldly asked the new company's president, Mitsunobu Kojima, for a special favor. Would he allow Tama to stay in Kishi Station?

It was an odd request, but Kojima wanted to help. And he had a good feeling when he met Tama. So he said yes! But how could he convince his employees and customers to accept keeping a cat around?

Kojima had an idea. He appointed Tama as official stationmaster, or creature in charge. Like his human employees, Tama went home every night. But whenever the calico cat was on duty, she stayed in a converted ticket booth equipped with a soft bed, cat tree, and high shelf. The booth sat near the entrance to the station and had big windows so Tama could see out and visitors could see in.

Of course, the furry railroad boss had to look the part. So she wore a collar, with an attached badge, and a handmade hat identical to those worn by human employees. Tama didn't mind—her owner trained her to wear hats when she was a kitten. In fact, she usually wore her miniature chapeau at an impossibly cute, jaunty angle.

Several times each day, a human employee took Tama from her window office and set her on a wooden platform to greet visitors and pose for photos. The patient kitty let strangers touch and stroke her, no matter how many there were.

*Tama and Kojima (holding Tama's successor) in a railway window.*

*This* maneki-neko, *which looks like Tama, is thought to bring good luck.*

And the public "lapped" it up. Ridership increased. Sales of Tama-themed items in the gift shop skyrocketed. Business improved so much that, in 2010, Kojima hired industrial designer Eiji Mitooka to remodel the exterior of the station. Inspired by Tama, Mitooka redesigned it in the shape of a cat's face! Inside the building a Tama-themed café sells cat-shaped cakes, and painted paw prints parade across the floor.

Mitooka even redecorated the company's three trains. He made a Strawberry Train, Toy Train, and, of course, a Tama Train. On that one, cartoon images of Tama dance across the sides of the railcars.

Together with the splendid station redo and 70 annual, company-sponsored special events, Tama rejuvenated the railway. It was like the old days. "There are stories from ancient times of cats saving people's lives and of cats that bring good luck," says Yamaki. Because of this, many Japanese people display ceramic statues of *maneki-neko*, or "beckoning" cats, in their homes and businesses. Tama's fans considered her a real-life good luck charm.

Tama continued drawing crowds until 2015. That

summer the elderly, but long-lived, 16-year-old cat passed away. Because many Japanese follow the Shinto religion, a sorrowful Kojima held a Shinto funeral service for her. Three thousand people attended! The beloved cat was buried in a shrine and pronounced a goddess in the Shinto belief, which honors many gods, including animal ones.

What began as an excuse to keep Tama in the railway station turned into an enormous tourist attraction. Because of her, other cats, a dog, and even a rabbit have been appointed stationmasters at other Japanese railways.

"Tama was an angel of the gods," says Yamaki. No doubt many would agree. ●

## ASK AN **EXPERT**

**Q:** Why are some cats more affectionate than others? What's the trick to raising a friendly cat?

**DR. WEITZMAN:** The friendliest cats are born to friendly, outgoing parents. And they are well-socialized as kittens. To socialize a kitten, you must gently handle and play with her every day—even if for only a few minutes—between the ages of two and eight weeks. This is also the time to expose her to different people, places, and animals. If you do all this during that window of opportunity, even a kitten born to a fearful mother is likely to grow up friendly and confident.

# BODY
## Language

Cats "talk" all the time. But they don't use words. They communicate with scent, sound, and body language. Kittyspeak is subtle but can be fun to learn. Check out these common poses and what they mean.

### FRIENDLY:

When a cat is glad to see you, she'll hold her tail straight up in the air and greet you with a cheerful sounding meow. Head-butting usually follows. Or she may rub her body back and forth against your legs.

### ANGRY OR AGGRESSIVE:

Beware of a cat that arches her back and fluffs up her tail. She's trying to look big and scary. If she's really mad, she'll also growl or screech, swing her tail, swivel her ears, and stare at you.

124

## FRIGHTENED:

A scaredy-cat's whole body gets tense. He tries to look small by tucking in his tail, flattening his ears, pulling back his whiskers, and ducking his head. Then he either crouches down or runs and hides.

## ALERT:

"Who goes there?" Even when sleeping, cats remain alert to any strange sound. If they hear one, their muscles tense and they perk their ears. A curious cat also may twitch her ears and her tail. But she stays focused on listening and won't make a peep herself.

## HAPPY:

Droopy whiskers; a loose, relaxed body; half-perked ears; blinking eyes; and soft (maybe quite loud) purring are the signs of a contented cat. And if you hold one on your lap, you'll feel happy, too.

CURIOUS

# LEO

## BIG CAT WITH A BIG HEART

*Lion/Kruger National Park, South Africa*

Lions are born to be free, not caged up as pets. "But lions are far more than a fierce, wild cat," says Karin Kruger. "They really shower you with affection." This is easy to see in hand-raised lions. And it doesn't mean that lions aren't dangerous. They are, and humans must never disturb one while eating, or give it any reason to feel afraid.

Karin knows. She grew up in South Africa's Kruger National Park, which was named after one of her ancestors. Her father served as game ranger there. One day, he heard a newborn lion cub crying for its mother. When the mama lion failed to return

## YOU CAN TELL LIONS APART BY THE SPOTS AT THE BASE OF THEIR WHISKERS.

after 24 hours, Karin's father brought the tiny baby home. Her mother made him a bed out of a cardboard box and bottle-fed him modified puppy formula. They called him Leo.

Until he was five months old, Leo lived like a house cat. Then he started ripping up pillows and chewing on the couch. "He would open the fridge and eat whatever he wanted," Karin says. "He was causing complete havoc." So the family shooed the lion outside. But then he sat by the door and cried. Lions are more social than leopards, tigers, and house cats. In the wild, they must live in family groups, or prides, in order to survive. It was only natural that Leo felt lonesome.

When Karin came home from boarding school on weekends, Leo was so happy to see her that he ran into her arms and licked her face. "He hated sleeping alone," she says. "He wanted me to sleep on his tummy, and he would put his paw on me." All that cuddling comforted Leo, but it gave Karin fleas! "It was awfully embarrassing," she says, "because everybody at school knew." Even the boys!

During the day, Karin and Leo played lion games. She rolled a car tire for him to chase. And when he was small, they often played tag. Leo would race after Karin trying to catch her or trip her with his paw.

But when Karin tried to train him to do what she said, Leo refused. He came when called, and that was it. "I tried to teach him to sit," Karin says. "But he would just look at

*Smile, please! BFFs Wolfe, Karin, and Leo pose for a touching group portrait.*

*The always affectionate Leo enjoys headbutting his favorite human, Karin.*

me, with this expression in his eyes that seemed to say he was king of the world. Then he would just stroll off."

However, Karin outsmarted the lion king. Leo often hung out with her dog, Wolfe, and mimicked everything Wolfe did. So Karin learned to make Leo sit by telling the dog to do it. She used this same technique when she tried, with hysterical results, to teach the lion to hunt. Every weekend, Karin took both animals on a walk to find a herd of impalas. When she spotted them, Karin told Wolfe to sit and stay, and Leo plopped down beside him. Then she circled around upwind of the herd and chased them toward the waiting "hunters." Karin hoped Leo would leap up and chase the prey. But he never did. "He would just lie there, panting with his mouth open, and watch the show," she says. Not until he saw Karin coming did he flatten his ears, crouch, and pounce ... on her!

Leo pulled a similar stunt whenever Karin's whole family went for a stroll. He would wait until the humans were relaxed and chatting. Then he would sneak ahead and hide in the tall grass. When his people got close, Leo jumped out at them, giving everyone a huge fright!

The playful cub never did learn to hunt. So he couldn't survive in the wild. Eventually, the Krugers gave him to a big cat sanctuary, where he lived a long life and fathered 18 cubs. But the lovable lion never forgot his human family. "Even years after he had his own pride," says Karin, who is now known as a wildlife artist, "Leo was overjoyed to see us." ●

# African Lion

🐾 **HOMELAND:** Sub-Saharan Africa

🐾 **DISTINGUISHING FEATURES:** Males boast shaggy collars of long hair called manes and can weigh as much as three grown men.

🐾 **WORTH KNOWING:** A lion can hear another lion roar up to five miles (8 km) away and tell if it is male or female, friend or foe.

# BUBBA

## PURR-FECT ATTENDANCE
### *Domestic Shorthair/San Jose, California, U.S.A.*

How do you choose a cat? Patrick Marienthal, of San Jose, California, went by color. Since he'd had super friendly, easygoing orange cats in the past, he wanted another. His wife, Amber, and their sons, Matthew and Mark, agreed.

So when California's San Jose Animal Care Center rescued a six-month-old, orange and white kitten off the street, the family pounced. They adopted him and named him Bubba.

But once they brought their new pet home ... holy moly! The former stray did nothing but yowl to go outside. "He nearly drove me insane," says Amber, who finally relented and opened the door. The minute

FOUR OUT OF FIVE ORANGE CATS ARE MALE. **MANY PEOPLE, INCLUDING VETERINARIANS, BELIEVE THAT ORANGE CATS ALSO INHERIT A "FRIENDLY" GENE** LINKED TO THEIR COAT COLOR.

she did, Bubba shot across the grass and bounded right over their high wooden fence. That fence separates the Marienthals' backyard from the sprawling campus of Bret Harte Middle School—where Matthew attended school—and Leland High School.

Both buildings are single-story, with multiple doors opening to the outside. This made it easy for a curious cat to find a way in. Even so, Amber was surprised when the middle school secretary called. "Your cat is in the principal's office," she said. And that was just the first of many more phone calls to come!

When Matthew moved up to Leland, Bubba moved up, too. Math. Chemistry. Library. Choir. During classes, the snuggly-soft "teacher's pet" could be found cat-napping most anywhere in the high school. Between classes, he served as self-appointed hall monitor.

And did he race for the door when the dismissal bell rang? Not this sports-minded tabby. He attended cheerleading practice, hung out in locker rooms, and sat in the stands during football games. Bubba stayed after school so often he deserved extra credit! So many people called Amber to report finding her "lost" cat that she had an elastic collar custom-made, with a message printed on it. The message read, "Harte and Leland. He's okay here."

And he was, until Amber and Patrick went to a wedding in Florida, leaving Amber's mother in charge at home. That Friday night, Bubba found himself accidentally locked inside Leland High. Luckily, Mark's friend walked by and heard the cat crying. The friend texted an alert that eventually reached the overnight school safety superintendent, who hurried to let Bubba out.

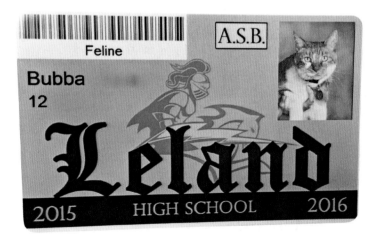

*Bubba may be the only cat in America with his own student ID card.*

Critter Camp, Petpals, Wild Careers, or Camp Vet. The programs go by many names, but there are hundreds of them scattered across the United States. Sponsored by Humane Society chapters, animal shelters, and branches of the Society for the Prevention of Cruelty to Animals (SPCA), they offer an exciting alternative to traditional summer day camps.

Fur-get swimming or basketball. These camps are all animals all the time, with the focus on dogs, rabbits, and ... cats. Lots of cats. Campers learn how to care for them, understand them, and keep them safe. Sometimes kids take complete charge of an animal for the week.

But the best camps give older kids a taste of what it's like working as a vet tech, animal rescue worker, or animal control officer.

At the Humane Society of Sarasota County, in Sarasota, Florida, about half the kids have animals at home when they start camp. When camp ends, that percentage jumps to two-thirds. Why? Once they make a new furry friend, some kids can't leave camp without him.

# SUMMER CAT CAMP

Other times, the confident kitty showed impeccable comic timing. On career day, a vet came to school to talk about her profession. And as if on cue, Bubba showed up and strutted across the stage during her speech!

The furry socialite also sometimes toured the neighborhood. Occasionally, he even spent the night in other people's yards. One neighbor let her own two cats outside and drove away for the day, only to return to find that Bubba had sneaked inside her house. He was gobbling up her cats' food, while her two disgruntled pets watched helplessly from out on the deck. "Bubba is fearless," Amber says. "This is his world, and he knows it."

When she tried keeping him home at night by blocking his cat door with a box, Bubba simply pushed the box aside. So Amber began adding weights. It took 50 pounds (23 kg) to keep Bubba confined!

Then something happened that turned Bubba into what the Marienthals call a "celebrikitty." Near the end of summer vacation, students had to report to school to have their photo IDs taken. Bubba, of course, stood first in line. Spotting a handy test subject, the photographer scooped him up and made a sample ID.

"That's my cat!" exclaimed Matthew when he saw it. He photographed Bubba's ID card with his camera phone and sent the photo to his mom, who posted it online. *Swish!* The post went viral, prompting a call from a national morning talk show the very next day.

Will this now famous student ever graduate? He may attend the ceremony, but one thing's for sure: Bubba is a smarty-cat. He knows school is cool, and likely will attend until he's old and gray. ●

# SNORRI

## NIGHT PROWLER

*Domestic Shorthair/Oregon, U.S.A.*

Burglars dress in black. They wear gloves and a ski mask and carry a pry bar. Right?

Not always. One famous robber in Portland, Oregon, commits his misdeeds wearing an orange fur coat. He prowls around on quiet, padded, kitty feet. And he doesn't need any burglar tools.

This sneaky crook is Snorri Sturluson. Named after a 12th-century Icelandic poet, he mostly steals footwear. Flip-flops are his favorite. But sticky-fingered, er, pawed Snorri has also made off with bath towels, Mickey Mouse ears, dog toys, gloves, a construction worker's knee pad, and a brand-new child's Halloween costume.

**BETTER HIDE YOUR RINGS IF YOU LIVE WITH AN AMERICAN BOBTAIL, BENGAL, MUNCHKIN, OR PIXIE-BOB CAT. THESE BREEDS ARE OFTEN JEWEL THIEVES THAT WILL STEAL ANYTHING SHINY THEY CAN GET THEIR PAWS ON.**

But, the first things Snorri stole were his owners' hearts. Medical student Gabrielle Hendel opened her front door one rainy day, and in trotted a beautiful, half-grown, orange tabby cat. Unable to find his owner, she kept him. "I was not a cat person," says Heather Olson, Gabbie's spouse. But sweet, huggable Snorri soon won her over.

Little did anyone know that beneath that charming exterior was the soul of a crook. Heather found a gardening glove lying in their backyard one afternoon and wondered where it came from. Then sheets of paper towels appeared. The mystery was solved when she spotted Snorri leaping over their fence with a paper towel clutched in his mouth.

Soon he began looking for better loot—and discovered footwear. Slippers. Sneakers. Boots. You name it. Snorri began hauling them home, sometimes one at a time, often in pairs. He somehow maneuvered an old, fur-lined leather boot with a heavy tread through his cat door and into the house. "He usually does this at night, when we're sleeping," Heather says.

The normally silent kitty drops his "booty" beside her bed and announces it with an odd sounding, extra-long meow. "He never makes a sound unless he has something," Heather says. Then he hops on the bed and demands to be petted.

Flip-flops are cheap. So Heather laughed off Snorri's shenanigans at first. But then he started bringing home expensive stuff—like children's shoes. To help people retrieve

*Lights, camera, action! A TV crew films Gabbie and Snorri for a local kitty, er, human interest news story.*

*Gabbie wheels a load of Snorri's loot around the neighborhood.*

their belongings, she started a social media account where she posts photos of the stolen goods for her neighbors to see. And once a month, she dumps all of Snorri's loot into a wheelbarrow and tours the neighborhood. At one house, the woman who lives there pulled out a surprising number of shoes. But then she dropped them right back on her front porch, where Snorri simply snitched them again.

Like most burglars, Snorri does most of his work after dark. But where does he go? Curious to find out, Heather and Gabbie attached a tiny, motion-activated, infrared camera (kitty cam) to the sneaky cat's collar. "It's really funny seeing the world through a cat's eyes," Heather says. They discovered that his territory encompasses a couple of city blocks. He usually travels through backyards, not on the sidewalks. And sometimes he comes face-to-face with other cats.

One video showed the real-life cat burglar avoiding the neighborhood fences and taking the long way home. Maybe he does that when he's carrying something heavy. Another one showed a knee-high view of the inside of a neighbor's garage littered with items ripe for the picking. But the biggest surprise occurred one night, when Heather and Gabbie took their dogs for a walk.

Reviewing Snorri's kitty cam footage afterward, they couldn't believe their eyes. Who did they see but themselves! "He was secretly following us and watching us," Heather says. "I knew about the shoes and the other cats, but I didn't suspect that!" And why would she? But that's all in a good night's work for Snorri Sturluson—robber, stalker, house cat, spy. ●

## ASK AN **EXPERT**

**Q:** How similar are domestic cats to wild cats?

**DR. WEITZMAN:** They're very similar. Wild cats helped Egyptians keep rodents out of their grain 10,000 years ago. But evidence suggests that it has only been 5,000 years since cats were commonly kept as pets. That's not long enough for house cats to lose much of their wild ways. Because of this, you can see all the same mannerisms and behaviors in our living room cats as you see in their much larger, wild relatives. It's just on a smaller scale.

# GEORGE

## STANDING TALL

*Minuet / Texas, U.S.A.*

Rhyan Patterson, 15, longed for a purebred Minuet kitty, which is a cross between a Munchkin and a Persian. "Please, please, please," she begged her parents, Andrew and Koa Park. Munchkin cats are an unusual breed. They have inherited a dominant gene that causes a type of dwarfism.

Named after the characters in *The Wizard of Oz*, the Munchkin breed officially began in 1983. That's when a snarling bulldog chased two pregnant, stray cats under a pickup truck. Music teacher Sandra Hochenedel hurried to help. After chasing the dog away, she lured the cats out with treats. Hochenedel then scooped them both up and

MINUET CATS USED TO BE CALLED NAPOLEONS. THE INTERNATIONAL CAT ASSOCIATION CHANGED THEIR NAME IN 2015 AND NOW CONSIDERS THEM A TOTALLY SEPARATE BREED.

carried them home. Later, she gave one away. The cat she kept she named Blackberry. When Blackberry had her kittens, a spontaneous mutation or genetic change occurred, and one kitten was born with very short, stubby, front legs. Hochenedel gave that kitty to a friend, who lived in Monroe, Louisiana, U.S.A. Before long, that cat began reproducing, and several short-legged kitties were seen running around Monroe.

Despite some people's fears, veterinarians found no evidence that the mutation harmed the cats. So The International Cat Association pronounced Munchkins an official breed in 2003. Other breeders began mating these new feline "dachshunds" to glamorous, long-haired Persians and created the Minuet. The Minuet has only been recognized as a breed since 2012! So they were rare and hard to get.

Rhyan's mother spent months searching, before she located a woman 200 miles (322 km) away, who had kittens for sale. Rhyan, her parents, and her two-year-old sister all drove out to get their new pet. Once there, the breeder handed Rhyan a yellow ball of fluff, with round eyes in a round face. Rhyan rubbed her cheek against the kitten's soft

*George uses his hind legs to get a better view while gazing out the window.*
*But he also sometimes assumes this position even when there's nothing to see.*

*Besides his upright stance, George has a funny habit of gurgling instead of meowing.*

fur and sighed. She was in love.

Rhyan named the kitty George, because the look on his face reminded her of an old man. As time passed, George grew, but his legs didn't; they stayed super short. George ran fast. He just couldn't jump very high.

Trouble was that George the vertically challenged cat was just as curious as Curious George, the storybook monkey. He always wanted to know what was going on, but he was too short to see. So if George heard a noise, like someone opening the front door, he surprised everyone by standing up on his hind legs to get a better look.

Before long, family members spotted George standing meerkat-like on the floor, the dining room table, and the back of Koa's office chair. At Christmastime, he posed still as a stuffed bear, on top of the packages under the tree. "All you could see was his chest moving in and out as he breathed," said Koa. "He didn't look real."

George looked so funny that Koa began posting pictures of him on social media. And people loved the stand-up cat. Within a week, George2Legs had over 10,000 followers online!

But George never let fame go to his head. He always put family first, perching on the arm of the couch whenever his people played board games or watched TV. "He is so entertaining that we can't help but laugh," Koa said. "He brings our family closer together."

Even the four-legged members. Besides George, the family has two regular house cats. One of them, Ruby, was so shy and skittish that she always hid. But after a year of watching George stand up in front of the refrigerator every morning to beg for a slice of ham, she came out of her shell.

Now, whenever George stands tall for his treat, so does Ruby.

Ruby is a champion copycat. But George is still the star of the show. ●

# Minuet

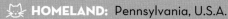 **HOMELAND:** Pennsylvania, U.S.A.

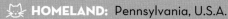 **DISTINGUISHING FEATURES:** Minuets look like feline dachshunds, with bodies like hot dogs and short, stubby legs.

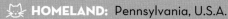 **WORTH KNOWING:** Minuets can do anything other cats can do, except maybe jump as high. Joseph B. Smith, an American Kennel Club dog show judge, created the breed in 1996.

# CAT
# PHOTOS
## How to take great ones

They're all over social media—supercute photos of supercute cats. But, hey! Your own cuddly kitty is just as sweet. If only you could manage to take a really great photograph of her. Well, you can. Just follow these tips:

### BRIBE HER WITH TREATS.

Professional animal trainers teach cat actors to stand on a mark by giving them goodies, usually tuna or ham. If you want Whiskers to pose for you, give her a taste of what is to come. Then hold a few treats in your hand while you take her picture. She gets those if she sticks around. You can also tape a treat to the top of your camera, or phone, to make her look up.

### SET THE STAGE.

Pretend you're doing an official photo shoot, and begin with the background. That should be simple: a rug or blanket in a color that complements Fluffy's fur will work. Think props next. If your kitty is a toilet paper fanatic, set a roll on the floor. You could also try an open box, catnip mouse, or smelly sock—whatever excites your pet.

## PAY ATTENTION TO LIGHTING.

The bright light of midday can cast weird shadows on things, so take your pictures in the morning or late afternoon. The light is softer then. Set up in a room that has a large window, open the drapes, and turn off your flash. The flash might spook your cat and can also make her eyes look red.

## ACTION SHOTS.

Dangle a piece of yarn or toss a toy in the air, and try to capture your cat acting natural. Try lying on your belly, so you and he are at eye level. You can even use a selfie stick to peer around corners or under the chair. Whatever you do, get close! Zoom in and focus right on your kitty's face. After all, she is adorable.

## TAKE LOTS OF PICTURES.

With digital photography, you don't have to pay for film. So go wild! If your camera phone has a burst mode, experiment with that. The more you click, the better your chances of getting a picture-purrfect shot.

# THE
# FINAL
# MEOW

"Way down deep, we're all motivated by the same urges. Cats have the courage to live by them."

—Jim Davis, creator of *Garfield*

# PAWS, LOOK & LEARN

## LEARN ABOUT CATS IN THE WILD

Blewett, Ashlee Brown. *Mission: Lion Rescue*. National Geographic, 2014.

Carney, Elizabeth. *Everything Big Cats*. National Geographic, 2011.

Hague, Bradley. *Rise of the Lioness*. National Geographic Kids, 2016.

Hoena, Blake. *Everything Predators*. National Geographic Kids, 2016.

Joubert, Dereck and Beverly. *Face to Face With Lions*. National Geographic, 2008.

Marsh, Laura. *National Geographic Kids Readers: Lions*. National Geographic, 2015.

## VIDEOS ABOUT FABULOUS FELINES

"Science of Cats" – National Geographic Channel, *Explorer*
A clip from a National Geographic Channel program, which shows viewers the latest scientific evidence revealing how cats set off on a journey to conquer the world.
channel.nationalgeographic.com/explorer/episodes/science-of-cats

*The Truth About Cats* – Nat Geo WILD
Making use of the latest technology, this Nat Geo WILD show explores the amazing world of cats, from how they communicate to their behaviors, and more.
channel.nationalgeographic.com/wild/the-truth-about-cats

"Can You Really Train Your Cat?" – National Geographic Kids
You may think your kitty companion can't be trained, but this circus troupe of well-trained cats is proof that even a stubborn kitty can learn new tricks.
natgeo.com/kids/trainyourcat

"Where Your Cat Goes May Shock You" – National Geographic Kids
A new study that placed GPS tracking devices on house cats turned up some interesting findings. While most cats stay in the vicinity of their homes, others travel much farther away, to the surprise of their owners.
natgeo.com/kids/cattravels

## ORGANIZATIONS THAT HELP CATS

There are lots of small cats out there that need homes, food, care, and love! And big cats are declining in numbers due to habitat loss and human activity. Check out the organizations below to learn more about these animals and ways that you can help them.

Animal Care Centers of NYC
nycacc.org

Edmonton Humane Society
edmontonhumanesociety.com/support-ehs

Good Samaritan Fund at Animal Emergency Hospital and Urgent Care, in Raleigh, North Carolina
ervets4pets.com

Hawaiian Humane Society
hawaiianhumane.org

Lil BUB's Big Fund for the ASPCA
secure.aspca.org/donate/lilbub

National Geographic's Big Cats Initiative
nationalgeographic.org/projects/big-cats-initiative

San Diego Humane Society and SPCA
sdhumane.org

San José Animal Care Center
sanjoseanimals.com

SMART Rescue
smartpetz.com

Seven Surprising Ways to Donate to Your Local Shelter
petfinder.com/helping-pets/information-on-helping-pets/unusual-donations-for-shelters-rescue-groups

## READ MORE ABOUT HOUSE CATS

Carney, Elizabeth. *National Geographic Kids Readers: Cats vs. Dogs.* National Geographic, 2011.

Miller, Kelley. *Just Joking Cats.* National Geographic, 2016.

Newman, Aline, and Gary Weitzman. *How to Speak Cat.* National Geographic, 2015.

Shepherd, Jack. *67 Reasons Why Cats Are Better Than Dogs.* National Geographic, 2014.

Spears, James. *Everything Pets.* National Geographic, 2013.

# Photo Credits

*To Neil, in honor of our 45th wedding anniversary.* —A. A. N.

Since 1888, the National Geographic Society has
funded more than 12,000 research, exploration, and
preservation projects around the world. The Society
receives funds from National Geographic Partners,
LLC, funded in part by your purchase. A portion of
the proceeds from this book supports this vital work.
To learn more, visit natgeo.com/info.

NATIONAL GEOGRAPHIC and Yellow Border
Design are trademarks of the National Geographic
Society, used under license.

For more information, visit nationalgeographic.com,
call 1-800-647-5463, or write to the following address:
National Geographic Partners
1145 17th Street N.W.
Washington, D.C. 20036-4688 U.S.A.

Visit us online at nationalgeographic.com/books

For librarians and teachers: ngchildrensbooks.org

More for kids from National Geographic:
kids.nationalgeographic.com

For information about special discounts for bulk
purchases, please contact National Geographic Books
Special Sales: specialsales@natgeo.com

For rights or permissions inquiries, please contact
National Geographic Books Subsidiary Rights:
bookrights@natgeo.com

Art directed by Julide Dengel
Designed by Ruth Ann Thompson

Trade hardcover ISBN: 978-1-4263-2734-6
Reinforced library edition ISBN: 978-1-4263-2735-3

Printed in China
17/PPS/1

The author and publisher would like to thank
everyone who worked to make this book come
together: Kate Hale, senior editor; Lori Epstein,
photo editor; Michelle Harris, researcher; Michaela
Weglinski, editorial assistant; Anne LeongSon and
Gus Tello, design production assistants; Grace Hill,
managing editor; Alix Inchausti, production editor.

# IF YOU LOVE KITTIES LEARN THEIR LANGUAGE!

Veterinarian and cat expert Dr. Gary Weitzman reveals how to communicate with your feline friend in this fun guide to decoding cat behavior, including wacky fun facts, training tips, vet and care advice, activities, quizzes, 100+ cat photos, and more.

## CaT TALK QUIZ

Test your kitty know-how! Match each cat's posture to the correct emotion. Fill in each box with the correct letter. (Check your answers below.)

1. **RELAXED** — "It's a calm, quiet day in the neighborhood."

2. **ANGRY** — "Get away! Or I'll make you leave!"

3. **FRIENDLY** — "Hi, there. You can pet me if you want."

4. **AFRAID** — "Come one step closer, and I'll bolt! I swear I will!"

5. **ANXIOUS** — "Uh oh. I don't think I'm going to like this."

6. **PLAYFUL** — "Come on. Shake a leg and play with me."

All cats pictured here are domestic shorthairs, except for C, which is a Peterbald.

Answers: 1.A, 2.C, 3.E, 4.B, 5.D, 6.F

14    15